HOW TO REALLY CHANGE YOUR LIFE

Discover Your Purpose, Unleash Your Potential, and Live Your Dream!

Norman Barlow, Ph.D.

How To Really Change Your Life
Discover Your Purpose, Unleash Your Potential, and
Live Your Dream!
by Norman Barlow, Ph.D.

Printed in the United States of America

ISBN 978-1-60477-059-9

Visit Norman Barlow's website at:
www.normanbarlow.com

www.xulonpress.com

Acknowledgements

I would like to thank my wife, Amy, for her patience, support, encouragement, and hours of work she has invested in the typing and editing this book.

I would like to acknowledge that except through the power and grace of God this book never would have been written nor would I have the energy to bring its powerful message to live audiences throughout the world.

Table of Contents

Introduction

Someone once said, "There are the winners in life, the losers in life, and those who have not yet learned how to win."

I believe that most of us want to be winners in life. However, most of us were never taught the secrets of personal achievement.

Think about it.

In all your years of being educated were you ever offered a course called *Success 101*?

Did anyone ever come along side and say, "I want to be your personal coach. I want to show you step by step how you can achieve your goals in life"?

Most of us go through our lives doing what we saw our parents do. We learned from their strengths, and we also picked up some of their weaknesses. Then most of us simply fumble through life "trying" different ways to change ourselves or achieve our goals only to fail several times.

Eventually we just stop trying. However, successful people know how to achieve the outcomes they want to experience in their life. They have discovered a system—a blueprint—they consistently use to achieve the results they desire.

Let me ask you a few questions:

What would you like to accomplish in your personal life right now?

What would you like to accomplish in your professional life right now?

Would you like to lose weight?

Increase your income?

Leave your dead-end, low paying job and start your own business?

Improve your relationships with others?

Start a new career?

Increase your sales?

Improve your performance or productivity?

Access more of your potential?

Begin creating the type of life you have always dreamed of living?

I believe each of us would like to change ourselves in some way. However, motivating ourselves to make those changes and making them stick is the real challenge.

Have you ever noticed how each time you say to yourself, "I am going to do something about..." related to changing some area of your life and yet you rarely remain committed long enough to reach your goal?

You are not alone.

In fact, 90% of those who begin any type of self-improvement program fail. You and I only have a 10% chance of following through with any type of positive change we set out to accomplish in our life.

In this book, you will learn how to motivate yourself and maintain your level of commitment until you achieve your goals. You will be given a blueprint—a step-by-step system—to follow that will help you move from where you are now to where you really want to go in life.

In this book I have included an exercise to complete that will give you insights into discovering your own unique purpose and destiny.

You will learn the secrets successful people know about personal achievement.

Changing your life takes much more than just talking about what you are going to do and getting all fired up about it. Change involves taking action.

There is a story about a couple who had just been married and who ran into some challenges on their wedding night. While they were getting ready for bed, the new bride was quite anxious.

"What is wrong, honey? Why are you nervous?" asked her husband.

"Well, I am a little nervous about tonight. You see, I haven't had relations with a man for a very long time," she replied.

"I can't understand that. You were married to your last husband for over twenty years before he passed away. Surely you were intimately involved with him throughout your marriage?" he asked.

"No, we never had intimate relations in all those years of marriage. You see, my former husband was a motivational speaker. Nothing physical happened. All he did was sit on the edge of the bed and talk about how good it was going to be!" she replied.

There are so many books and speakers who are out there telling you what you should be doing with your life. However, most of them do not give you the practical steps and techniques on how to actually do it!

Motivational speakers and "self-help gurus" talk a lot about "how good it is going to be". Then they let you down when it comes to that part about "how you can actually make these changes in your life".

In this book, you *will* find out the "How To" practical steps you need to take in order to make powerful changes in your life.

I won't let you down.

I will also be brutally honest with you and may even offend you at times. I will also share with you my own successes and failures.

Someone once said, "A smart person learns from their mistakes; however, a wise person learns from the mistakes of others."

Hey, guess what?

In this book, you can learn from mine.

Chapter 1

Where Are You?

Perhaps you are lying in bed and saying to yourself, "This is just another day that I have to get up and go to work—doing the same thing over and over again, going to a job with people who are negative, complaining, and toxic."

As you lie in bed, you think about getting your morning coffee to jumpstart your day.

You think about your future and feel hopeless, believing things will never change.

So here you are! Perhaps you have reached the height of your game. You have all the money you need and all the toys you could ever want, yet you still feel unsatisfied with your life. It seems as if this comfortable life you have just isn't cutting it anymore. There is a longing within you to venture down a new path. You know it has something to do with your life purpose and destiny and yet you have no idea what to do.

So here you are! You are working as a clerk in a department store or a fast food restaurant. People tell you that you could be doing so much more with your life and that you are living below your potential. You know in your heart you were born for more than this. You are frustrated working long hours in a low paying job wishing you could change your circumstances. However, you have no idea how to turn your frustration and discontentment into a powerful motivating force to move you toward a better life.

So here you are! You have spent most of your life wiping runny noses, dirty hands, cleaning up spills around the house, and driving kids from one event to the next. Now the children are grown up and no longer need you as much as they did when they were younger.

"Who am I? What is my purpose in life? What can I do about my feelings of loss, frustration, and boredom now that it seems as if the life I once had is gone?" These are questions you never had the time to ask yourself while taking care of your family—questions you would like to work toward knowing the answers to.

So here you are! You are overweight, out of shape, and have several medical complications .You feel sad and lonely, wishing that you could be active and involved in life, and food seems to be your only source of comfort.

You dream of changing your life for the better and yet it seems as if you are under some hypnotic spell that keeps you doing the same things every day that are destroying your health and your hope for the future. You feel angry, ugly, depressed, and frustrated all at the same time. You want to change your life, yet it seems as if there is no way out.

So here you are! You have become a certified professional victim of misfortune. Perhaps you have been jilted by someone you loved deeply who left you for another. Perhaps you were abused in some way. Perhaps you suffered some form of injustice.

Your experience has left you paralyzed in terms of moving on in your life. It seems as if you just simply exist, moving through your life carrying a big ball of hurt, pain, and anger.

Perhaps you have given up on the dreams you once had; the joy and laughter you once knew. Perhaps you are sitting on the sidelines of life just marking time instead of making your mark in the world.

So here you are! Perhaps you have moved from job to job, from relationship to relationship, from state to state, and from one dream to the next. It seems as if you are confused about what your purpose in life is and how you can stay disciplined long enough to live it out if even if you ever did discover it.

So here you are! You are looking at your life and you know this isn't the life you really want to be living. You are frustrated and angrily push yourself through each day knowing that you want something more and yet have no idea what it is. Perhaps you are taking your frustration out on your kids, your partner, or your co-workers.

It feels like the engine inside of you is revving up at full speed and you feel out of harmony within yourself. It feels like you are burning out on the inside. You say to yourself, "Something has to change in my life and yet I don't know which direction to go in and even if I did, I would have no idea how I could ever get there."

So here you are! You have a good job and only a few more years to "put in" before you get your pension. Life is pretty much predictable each day. Your only break from it all is the odd workshop you attend and your annual vacation to a warm place in the winter. You are simply putting in time waiting for the next event in your life to 'just happen'.

So here you are! Life is ticking by and you are in the same place today physically, spiritually, and economically as you were five years ago. You had a dream you wanted to pursue in life; however, you sold it out for a boring job, three hours of television a night, a bag of chips, and a diet soda.

"If I just numb myself to this longing buried deep within me to follow my dream in life, I'll be o.k.," you often think to yourself.

You are tired, depressed, and simply wait until bedtime since sleep is your only escape from the heartbreak of a dream that still lives within you waiting to be lived out.

So here you are! You know where you want to go in your life and exactly what you want to accomplish. You have a clear vision of who you want to become, what you want to have, and what you want to experience. However, you feel discouraged since you do not know how to get from where you are now to where you want to go.

Regardless of where you are at this moment in your life or which one of these situations you feel you might be able to relate to, I will show you how you can discover your unique purpose in life, turn fear, discontent, and frustration into powerful motivators, and how to transform the life you have into the life you want.

So, where are you now?

Are you willing to finish reading the rest of this book? Are you willing to follow a systematic approach to changing yourself and your life for the better? Or do you want to stay where you are?

The choice is up to you.

Chapter 2

Breaking Point

℘

**"People begin to become successful the minute
they decide to be." – Harvey Mackay**

The first step in changing either yourself or
your present circumstances involves making a
personal decision to commit yourself to achieving
the results you want to experience in your life.

At what point does your personal decision transform into a resolution?

When you finally wake up and say to yourself,
**"That's it. I am no longer choosing to live this
way anymore!"** You reach a boiling point in terms
of frustration and say, **"Enough is enough. I am no
longer going to be this way or live like this!"**

I came across an article in *Chatelaine* magazine
about several women who had succeeded at losing
weight. It seemed as if each of them had come to the

breaking point in their lives before they were motivated to make a change. In the article, *Chatelaine* records the story of one woman named Bonnie Gunther.

"Bonnie Gunther and her partner applied for life insurance. When the 34-year-old stepped on the scale for her medical, the doctor informed her she weighed 304 pounds. She cried as she left the office, but didn't do anything about losing weight. A few months later, Bonnie's own doctor diagnosed her with sleep apnea and suggested she lose weight for her health. 'I was finally ready to *do something* about my predicament other than cry.'"[1]

Most people have experienced a "breaking point" at some moment in their life. However, for most people that first experience just wasn't intense enough to motivate them to take consistent action to make significant, lasting changes.

When you reach your *true breaking point* you are ready to do something—anything—to change yourself or your situation.

Breaking point = The Place of Power

Breaking point is one way to reach a place of power. It is the moment that we wake up and finally *do something* either about ourselves or our situation.

We *make a decision*. We take *immediate action*. We use the *resources* we have at the time, no matter *where we are* or *what we have available*.

We take a positive step toward changing ourselves or our life in some way *despite how we feel*. We continue to make progress even though setbacks, obstacles, opposition, or difficult circumstances may arise.

Behaviour and Feelings

Some people wait until they "feel like doing something" before they take action. When you reach breaking point, your feelings do not matter. You take action despite how you feel physically or emotionally. You know that something must be done about your situation—no matter what.

Building Up To Breaking Point

Sometimes as feelings of frustration, hurt, or pain accumulate over time, they can either produce constructive or destructive results depending on how they are interpreted and channeled. Sometimes they build up to a breaking point as we formulate a picture of how things could be in our life rather than what they are presently.

For example, a sales representative for a large company discovers that each day he/she is becoming increasingly frustrated since they are only reaching marginal or average sales targets.

Their sales manager keeps applying pressure on them to "sell more" and "make more calls". They continue to do so seeing no results.

Finally, they come to the breaking point in which they say to themselves, "That's it! I am choosing to become the top sales representative in the company despite territorial issues, market trends, competition, and my past performance."

They see themselves receiving large commission cheques from their increased volume of sales.

They see themselves standing out from among the thousands of other sales representatives working for the company who remain unnoticed.

Somehow, they have hooked into the idea that "life is too short to be small," and they want to make a difference.

They reach a breaking point and ask to train and "job shadow" with the top sales representative in another branch .They "shadow" them and learn their techniques that have taken them to the top.

They take this step without pay and commit themselves to this training program.

They also hire a personal coach to help them recognize their unique strengths and weaknesses.

They return to their position and outsell everyone in their territory and spend a portion of their time helping other sales representatives improve their skills.

They now make fewer sales calls, have more free time, and are making more money.

How did they do it?

They saw a different picture of the type of life they wanted to have.

They came to the place of breaking point.

They discovered their unique strengths, skills, and abilities.

They were willing to pay the price to learn how to win at the game they wanted to play.

The Dog on the Porch Syndrome

One of the reasons why we seldom follow through with making changes in our lives is simply that we have grown accustomed to living with a certain level of pain. Our situation hasn't become unbearable enough to take action.

There is a story about a farmer who had a dog that was lying on the porch and was continuously howling.

A man passing by asked the farmer, "Why is your dog howling?"

"'Cause he is lying on a big nail coming up through the floor of the porch," the farmer replied.

"Why doesn't he get up off the nail?" the man asked.

"I guess he don't want to get up 'cause it just ain't painful enough," the farmer replied.

Norman, You Are Obese!

Several years ago, my doctor told me, "Norman, you are obese! You are at a severe risk of having a heart attack or stroke and dying." I remember crying all the way home from his office, thinking to myself, "I am a fat pig and I am going to die."

I said to myself, "That's it! I have got to do something about my weight or I am going to die. I **must** do something—anything—to get this weight off." I did not have a coffee and a donut on the way home from the doctor's office that day even though it was my usual stress response.

When you reach your breaking point, you often voice an internal or external statement or declaration that is brutally honest about yourself or your situation. You then agree with yourself to take immediate action to change yourself or your situation.

I made preparations the night before for the next morning. I found my sweat pants and an old pair of running shoes. I had them all ready to go. I set my alarm clock to get up early to begin walking. I set a goal of fifteen minutes per day and to lose ten pounds per month. (Consult with your family physician before you begin any type of weight loss or exercise program.)

When you reach your breaking point, you work with what resources you have available and set realistic and achievable goals. You make preparations in advance. You begin to make small consistent changes in your daily routines that will take you toward the results you are seeking to achieve.

I woke up the next morning and sat on the edge of my bed while everything within me was screaming, "Go back to bed where it is warm. Start walking tomorrow." I then said out loud, "I'm fat and I am going to die. I must lose this weight or I am going to be dead!"

When you reach your breaking point, you face the truth about yourself and your situation. You are brutally honest about your situation and the consequences you might experience if you fail to make a change. You declare this out loud, telling your brain and your being what is really taking place in your life.

I then ventured out into the cold, began to walk briskly while frequently checking my watch and wondering when this fifteen minutes of torture was going to end. I also weighed myself before I left home and kept a record of this in a little book tucked away in my nightstand.

When you reach your breaking point, you begin to take action to change yourself or your situation. You then find some method to measure your progress in order to know if you are reaching your set goal. The first step you take toward changing your life in a positive way will be difficult, and you may hate every minute of it.

Why?

Most of us resist change.

You will immediately create several reasons why you should give up and avoid changing. These reasons scream at you every step of the way for awhile as you develop new thinking patterns and behaviours.

After arriving home, I realized I had blood dripping down my leg. My big fat thighs had been rubbing together. As I walked, the friction between the two of them had created a chaffing effect, causing my inner thighs to bleed.

When you reach your breaking point and begin to take the very first active step toward making a positive change in your life, it seems as if immediately something will happen to influence you to think about sabotaging your goal. Be careful you do not develop the "I will wait until…" thinking. In my case, it would be, "I will wait until my chaffed porky thighs heal before I start my walking program."

The next morning before I went out for my walk, I coated the inside of my thighs with petroleum jelly to prevent them from chaffing and continued walking for my fifteen minutes.

When you reach your breaking point and you are committed to changing a certain area of your life, you will learn how to become resourceful and overcome obstacles that might keep you from making those changes. The pain associated to reaching the breaking point often makes people ingenious and creative when it comes to overcoming challenges. Recognize that the pain of staying the way you are or in the same situation is greater than the pain you experience attempting to make a change.

I then increased my walking from fifteen minutes to twenty and then steadily in increments of five minutes. I started reading about nutrition and vitamins that would help me improve my personal health. I picked up the *Alive Magazine* from a local health food store each month.

When you reach your breaking point, take action, and gain a small victory in one area of your life, you will often want to expand into different areas that are in congruency with your overall objective.

My walking then led to jogging for about forty minutes per day, and I was losing the weight. I woke up each morning saying to myself, "I love to jog each day. I feel great and look great!"

Negative affirmations that are brutally honest can often initially motivate us to change. When we do experience progress, we can honestly create positive affirmations that reflect this reality in our lives. Affirmations without action create a state of self-delusion.

Why Do We Stay Where We Are?

I believe there are eleven reasons why we do not move from where we are now in our lives to where we want to go. They are:

1. We think that things will just magically get better by themselves in time.

Have you ever heard someone say any of the following? "Don't worry about it." "Everything will work out for the best." "Just carry on the way you are." "There is a silver lining in every cloud." Listen, if I'm told my town is going to be flooded, I am not going to wait for the flood to come and then look for the silver lining in the storm cloud. I would either leave town or buy a big boat. Don't believe this irrational thinking that things get better if you neglect them and that you do not need to take action to improve or change your situation. The only thing that gets better on its own in time is a bottle of wine.

2. We are waiting for someone to come along and rescue us from our situation.

Some people are waiting for someone else to step in and help them change their situation. They complain about their situation and tell everyone how horrible it is, hoping that someone will jump in and rescue them. People who constantly rescue others are called "enablers". In their attempt to provide continual support, they often prevent others from developing self-reliance.

3. **We constantly look for ways to reframe and reinterpret our situation without taking any active steps to change it.**

Have you ever heard people say, "Look on the bright side," or "See the glass as being half full rather than half empty"? Yes, there are some benefits to changing the interpretation we attach to certain things and seeing things from a positive perspective. However, sometimes we attach positive meanings to situations so we can remain stuck in them. Since we have attached a new positive interpretation to our situation, we are now off the hook in terms of taking any action to change it. An example of this is someone reframing the fact that their business is going bankrupt, saying to themselves, "I will just let this happen and let it take its course. Just think how much better I will be able to empathize with others who have experienced financial shipwreck." In this case, they may find it easier to reframe their situation and remain in it instead of taking action to salvage their company.

4. We are trapped in a state of waking hypnosis in which we just accept things the way they are even if they are getting worse.

I remember hearing a rattling sound from under the hood of my car. It didn't seem too bad so I left it. In time, the noise became louder. What did I do? I turned my radio up to drown out the noise. The rattling under the hood became even louder. What did I do? I turned up my radio even louder. In the end, my water pump gave out, my engine blew up, and it cost me $2300.00 to have a rebuilt engine installed.

Sometimes we know something isn't going right in our lives, and we simply just let it continue. It seems as if we become paralyzed into a state of not caring about what happens to us. We "turn up" the volume of our lives in several ways to live in a state of delusion or denial and keep rolling along day to day.

How do we get out of this state of waking hypnosis in which it seems as if we are robots just moving through life marking time?

First, take some time away to be alone and take an inventory of your life. I mean book a hotel room for a day and night and just sit in the quietness of that space and review your current life away from all the distractions.

Secondly, write down how your life would be different if it could be. Allow yourself to relax, rest, and dream.

Thirdly, look at areas that drain you in your day to day life and look at the different options and alternatives you can choose from to either eliminate them or change your response to them to manage your own personal energy level more effectively. Don't wait for life's wake-up calls from the front desk!

In my experience, life's wake-up calls are startling and can send us reeling. Wake yourself up to the reality of your own life. Face the truth brutally and honestly and then set a course to change your life into what you want it to be.

5. **We believe that the pain associated to changing is greater than the pain we are experiencing by staying where we are. We may also have a painful association connected to changing a certain aspect of our lives due to a past negative experience.**

Once, I had a terrible tooth infection. I decided that it was better to keep popping pills to numb the pain than to have the tooth examined. I believed it was more torture to go to what I called "The House of Pain" rather than to put up with the constant ache caused by the infection. Perhaps this fear was instilled during my childhood. As a child, I had a dentist who, in my mind, looked like a character from a horror movie who worked in a bizarre laboratory filled with tools used for torture. My past painful experiences of going to the dentist as a child influenced me to remain in my present situation as long as I could. I saw going to the dentist to have my tooth looked at and possibly removed as being more painful than enduring the constant dull ache.

6. **We perceive that we live in a state of constant crisis. We are thus unable to take steps toward changing our lives since we are always in a crisis management mode.**

In working with people who want to quit smoking, I discovered that many of them had an excuse why "right now" was not a good time to quit. They planned to quit as soon as things became less stressful in their life. Guess what? Things never become less stressful. These people never came to the place of breaking point since they always had a crisis to be resolved **before** they could "work on" quitting their habit.

Most people who believe they are living in a state of constant crisis find it difficult to make the commitment to change. They are easily distracted by everyday events and are unable to make a decision to change some aspect of their life that could impact them positively for a lifetime.

Sometimes we can become "crisis conscious". It seems as if we interpret everything as being a crisis and respond to it in such a way. This sense of being "crisis conscious" is a cleverly devised technique some of us use to avoid taking the risks and disciplined actions connected to changing our lives.

7. We have bought into the "acceptance" and "gratefulness" theories that teach us to simply accept ourselves as we are. We are to be grateful for our current circumstances, even if we are unhappy.

I have some issues with these 'body image' folks who teach people to simply accept themselves being grossly overweight while they are on the road to deteriorating health and possibly an early death.

I have some issues with being told to be grateful for a miserable life when each of us can do something to improve our situation.

The "acceptance theory" often gives people the justification they need to give up working toward improvement.

A close cousin to the "acceptance theory" is what I call "being labeled". Most people live up to the labels that some professional has placed upon them. I have seen this in the field of psychiatry. It seems as soon as some people get their diagnosis, they begin to research it on the internet and live out the symptomatology associated with it to an even greater degree. It almost seems as if to some they have found their "niche" in life and sometimes substitute it as their purpose in life. For some there is a sense of relief since they can now live out what they believe is their purpose in life by living up to the label they have been given.

8. **We have a low self-esteem and have failed so many times in the past in our attempt to make changes that we cannot afford to fail again. We no longer believe the promises we make to ourselves since we have broken them so many times. We may also fear receiving rejection and ridicule from others if we work toward changing our lives in a positive way.**

Where does building self-esteem really begin?

It begins by keeping the most important promises we can make—the ones we make to ourselves. Our self-esteem begins to rise when we take action to honor those promises.

Building your self-esteem through a 'touchy feely,' 'let's all give each other a pat on the back' approach doesn't last. Affirmations are nothing more than well-crafted delusions unless they lead to action.

The mutual admiration society produces a lot of fluffy 'feel goods' that float away. Keeping the promises we make to ourselves, taking action, and seeing results is really the secret key to building and maintaining one's self-esteem.

How can you build your own self-esteem?

Here is the answer in a nut shell.

Tonight before you go to bed, write out a list of three goals you will achieve the following day. Make them simple and attainable. Then, review your wins at the end of the day before you go to bed that night and set for yourself three more goals for the next day.

When you write down your small wins, you cannot only see your progress, you will build integrity with yourself in terms of keeping the promises you have made to yourself.

Keeping the small promises we make to ourselves helps us to build the muscle we need to keep the bigger ones we would like to make in the future.

When it comes to receiving rejection or ridicule from others as we decide and work toward changing our lives, here is the raw truth. It will most likely happen!

The only way to overcome ridicule and rejection is to become inoculated against it. It is to become so immune to it that it has no power over you.

I recall wanting to be a magician, performing shows for young children. The very first show I did I burned my finger, cut my hand, and dropped half the props on the stage. I was so nervous that very few tricks worked and the children were amused yet not entertained.

The man who booked me for the children's show hired me since I charged about $50.00 and told him I was just learning how to perform magic for children. After the disastrous performance he said, "You are the worst magician I have ever seen. I would never book you again. You might as well quit and get out of magic. It's not your thing."

For days I felt sick to my stomach and wondered how much I could get if I sold all my store-bought props.

Then, I decided to call the man up and thank him. Yes, thank him! "I would like to thank you for giving me the opportunity to try out my tricks and learn from the experience. I realize I need improvement, and I was glad to have the chance to perform," I said.

I then went on to perform some more disastrous magic shows until I developed my skills to the point where I was making $500.00 per show, performing for service clubs, company picnics, and outdoor special events.

The best way to get over rejection and ridicule is to get a good steady dose of it until it no longer affects you. Turn it around and use it to increase your drive and commitment to achieving the outcomes you desire.

Being unwilling to pay the price of looking foolish, being ridiculed, being rejected, and learning through failure after failure are some of the reasons why most people never go beyond merely dreaming about changing their lives in a powerful and significant way.

9. **We take the advice of a so-called expert that tells us what we want to hear. This gives us the excuse we are looking for in order to avoid making changes in our lives.**

Once, a 200 pound woman and an out of shape man told me how they had heard on the radio that eating dark chocolate was good for our health. They went on to explain how the dark chocolate helps put you in a good mood and how it is healthy for your heart. They then justified eating chocolate bars on a regular basis since they believed a so-called expert telling them chocolate was good for them.

People who don't want to change will often find experts and websites that will tell them exactly what they want to hear in order to justify their behaviours.

There is a story about a nomad who was traveling across the desert and ran out of food. The only thing he had left to eat was a bag of figs. While in his tent under candle light, he began to eat his figs, enjoying every bite. Suddenly, he felt something in his mouth. He stuck his finger in the side of his mouth and pulled out a beetle. He sorted through the bowl of figs to discover they were infested with beetles. He then blew out the candle and continued to eat the rest of the figs.

For some of us, it is easier to dim the light of truth bearing on our situation and find someone or some way to justify our current course of action. This often seems a whole lot easier than changing ourselves or our direction in life.

10. We don't know how to succeed at making lasting changes in our lives.

Isn't it amazing how we, as parents, will invest all kinds of time, energy, and money into our children to teach them how to win at sports? However, we are reluctant to spend money on a book, CD, MP3 download, or seminar to help ourselves in order to help them win at achieving their goals in life.

Isn't it interesting how each year we will spend money maintaining our hair; and yet, we are reluctant to spend money in the area of personal development? I mean, we spend more money taking care of the outside of our head than we will taking care of the inside of our head

I recently attended a presentation in which the poverty of a particular area in Ontario, Canada, was addressed. I listened to the speaker talk about all the things the government was doing to help these people in poverty, basically enabling them to remain in their state of learned helplessness.

Finally, I could take it no more.

I raised my hand and asked the question, "Do you know of any program that will teach those in poverty how to live in abundance and attract wealth into their life? Is there a program in which people who were once in poverty overcame it, and how they might be a role model and teach those in poverty how to do the same?"

I received a vague answer and comments how such a program wouldn't work.

I like what Jim Rohn said. "Formal education will make you a living; self education will make you a fortune."

I believe teaching our children and teen-agers how to educate themselves in the area of self-improvement and providing them training in the area of how to win at the game of life would decrease some of the negative outcomes taking place in our local communities.

11. We are being "enabled" in some way.

Some people may find it difficult to change if someone or some organization is supporting them in their self-destructive choices, lifestyle, or behaviours.

Enablers are those who, by their interventions, keep those they assist in a state of what is called "learned helplessness". Enablers take care of other people and their problems and help clean up the consequences of their actions. Enablers are the kind of people who keep giving others money instead of teaching them how to earn it for themselves.

I recall as a boy wanting a bike like every other kid on the street. I asked my dad if he would buy me one. I had a picture of a wonderful father and son moment going to Consumers Distributing, filling out the little form with the small sawed-off pencil, and seeing the clerk produce a large box containing my brand new bicycle.

"I will pay 50% of the cost of any bike you want. You have to think of a way to make the other 50%," was my father's response. "How can I make the money?" I asked.

My dad went around to the backyard and brought out a manual push mower and rake. "Son, I want you to sit on the porch all day long if you have to and think about how you can use these to make money for that new bike you want," he said as he left for work.

In an hour, I was knocking on doors in the neighbourhood asking people if they needed their lawn cut. I earned my 50% and bought the bike. I also learned how much my father loved me since during my childhood he instilled in me the principle of taking action to get what you want rather than whining about it until others do it for you.

How Can We Get Ourselves to Experience a Personal Breaking Point?

If reaching breaking point is one way to motivate ourselves to make positive significant changes in our lives, then how do we get there?

1. Think about the situation that is causing you a tremendous amount of pain or frustration in your life right now that you would like to change.

2. Imagine seeing in your mind (as if you were watching a movie) all the painful and frustrating moments connected to the situation. Think about how much joy, money, time, energy, and opportunities that have been negatively affected or lost due to this situation. Imagine moments when this

situation has negatively affected those you love as well.

3. As you review each event, feel the feelings of pain and frustration connected to each of these scenarios. Remember the pain and frustration you felt during those times.

4. Hear any words, phrases, or things that were said to you connected to the events that caused you to feel a sense of pain and frustration.

5. Now imagine the various scenes fading in and out with full colour and sound. Notice how the images become bigger and brighter. Experience any sounds, smells, or feelings to an even greater degree.

6. Now answer these questions to yourself. "Do I really want to continue to live like this?" "What will my future hold if I continue on in this way?" Hear these words as a voice within you—a voice calling out for an answer. Then, if you truly believe it is crucial that you change this area of your life and take action to do so, move on to step 7.

7. Take your hands and clap them together, saying out loud, "**That's it! I have had enough. Once and for all and forever I am making a change. I am choosing to change this area of my life for good!**"

8. Now think about one thing you can do **immediately** to prove to yourself that you are **totally committed** to the process of making a powerful and lasting change in this area of your life. **Then do it.**

9. Now, whenever you feel apathetic or feel as if you are falling back into a rut, or if your level of self-motivation seems to be decreasing, immediately repeat this exercise.

Summary of How to Reach the Breaking Point

T - **Think** about something in your life that is causing you pain or frustration.

H - **Have mental pictures** of times in your life in which you have become frustrated or hurt as a result of being in particular situations.

R - **Review** each of these painful and frustrating moments, feeling the intensity of the emotions connected to the frustration and pain.

E - **Enter** into these scenarios any words or phrases that possibly someone else or others have said that caused you frustration or hurt feelings.

S - **See** the different scenarios fading in and out slowly. See them becoming bigger and brighter. Feel the feelings associated with them. Notice any sounds, smells, or tastes connected to the moments of frustration or pain.

H - **Honestly** ask yourself, "Do I really want to continue to experience these outcomes in my life?" "What will my future hold for me if I continue to live this way?"

O - **Open** your hands and then clap them together, saying out loud, "**That's it. I have had enough. Once and for all and forever I am making a change. I am choosing to change this area of my life for good.**"

L - **List** on a sheet of paper as many things you can do right now to take immediate action to begin changing your situation.

D - **Decide** to take action immediately and **do** something to let your brain know you are committed to changing this area of your life.

Chapter 3

Become Clear and Focused About What You Want

"Our plans miscarry because we have no aim.
When a man does not know what harbor he is
making for, no wind is the right wind." — Seneca

After reaching breaking point and knowing exactly what you don't want to experience in your life, the next step is to become clear and focused in terms of knowing exactly what you do want. I came across this excellent metaphor at a training seminar. Unfortunately, its source is unknown.

Ogson: His Story

Once upon a time, an upper echelon sales director sent a directive to all his sales managers. It said: "The quota for this quarter is $1,000,000. I know you can do it! Sell! Sell! Sell!"

Upon receiving this directive, local managers held motivational meetings for their sales people. They said, "The quota for this quarter is $1,000,000. You are the greatest sales people this company ever had, so get out there and sell, sell, sell! You can do it!" Furthermore, they advised each sales person to: "Cut out a picture of the one thing you would like to own by the end of the quarter and put it above your desk so you will be reminded each day of what you are working for. Now, go get'em!"

Ogson left the meeting highly motivated. "I am a great salesman, and I am going to earn a lot of money," he said aloud to himself. He cut out a picture of a very expensive car, and as he put it above his desk, he told himself, "That's what I'm working for." Ogson put his sales kit in his very best attaché case, dressed himself in his finest clothing, and pedaled off on the fastest company bicycle.

Although Ogson was unaccustomed to the twists and turns of the road, he nevertheless pedaled with all his might. However, during one foggy stretch of road, Ogson unavoidably rode the bicycle into a ditch. Ogson sadly left the twisted wreck upside down with its wheels spinning uselessly. After walking but a few steps, he tripped over a partially buried object. It was an ancient bottle. When Ogson removed the stopper, a gaseous cloud spewed forth from the brass bottle and formed itself into a Jinn, who asked,

"Where are you going?"

"I'm going out to make a lot of money selling," replied Ogson, confidently.

"You are fortunate," said the Jinn. "For letting me out of the bottle, I'll give you a winged horse so you'll be able to get there a lot faster."

"That's wonderful," said Ogson, who mounted the winged horse and flew off much faster than before. However, perhaps because he once worked in the center ring of the circus, the winged horse could only fly in circles. Not being satisfied with this, Ogson again called for the Jinn.

Somewhat annoyed, the Jinn said, "For letting me out of the bottle, I'll give you my magic carpet so you will be able to go even faster."

So Ogson sped along faster than ever. The ride, however, was quite erratic. The carpet would unexpectedly change direction—left, right, up, down. Ogson thought the ride was very much like being on a roller coaster. Unsatisfied with the progress he was making, Ogson again called upon the Jinn.

Very annoyed, the Jinn said, "Enter my bottle, and you will make instantaneous progress."

"That's great," said Ogson, and quickly entered the brass bottle. The Jinn put the stopper back on the bottle and Ogson was never seen or heard from again.

There are a number of morals to this fable. For example, one might be: If you are not clear as to where you are going or how best to get there, you may well end up someplace else.

The Three Percent Club

Did you know that only 3% of all people have written goals and know where they are going in their life?

Did you know that 10% of the general population dream about changing their life in some way and think about their future periodically?

Did you know that 87% of the general population live their lives without any specific goals and have no definite plan for their future? [2]

Discovering what you want out of life will get you into the 3% club. However, most of us have never been taught how to figure out what we want in life or how to discover our personal destiny.

Designing Your 'Future Self'

University psychologist, Hazel Markus, conducted research in the field of exploring our "future selves". This involved seeing images of who we might become and what we might look like in the future. In one study, college students were asked to choose from 150 possible descriptions when imagining their "future selves". When asked to describe themselves in the present, they chose 51 descriptions. When asked to construct a picture of what they would look like in the future, they chose an average of 80 descriptions with some choosing as many as 147. Almost half of them chose all 50 of the positive descriptions when creating a picture of their "future selves". [3]

I believe that most of us could create a picture of who we would like to be in the future, and, in most cases, we would choose descriptions that would be positive and push us beyond who we currently think we are.

Looking Within—Discovering Direction in Your Life and Defining Changes

Here is a practical technique drawn from the teachings of solution focused therapy that will help you discover some direction in your life. Most people, if they simply took enough time to reflect upon who they would like to be and how they would like their lives to be different, could develop a future picture of some kind.

'The Life You Have Always Dreamed of Living' Exercise

Find yourself a comfortable, quiet place where you can be alone. Close your eyes and take ten deep breaths, relaxing yourself. Then do the following exercise.

Imagine yourself climbing into bed, ready to have a restful and peaceful sleep. Imagine falling into a deep sleep. While you are asleep, something mysterious takes place.

It seems as if while you were sleeping, your life was being transformed.

Imagine yourself awakening in the morning. You notice that there is something very different about this particular morning. You sense something you may have not experienced in your entire life. You feel alive, energized, optimistic, and enthusiastic about waking up and living out the day.

While you were sleeping, your life changed. It has become the type of life you have always dreamed of living. You can hardly believe it is true; yet it is.

You get out of bed and begin to live out this wonderful day of your new life. It is almost as if you have had a rebirth of some kind. You see yourself doing what you have always wanted to do, having what you always wanted to have, and being the person you have always wanted to be.

You are so different.

You look different. You act different. It seems as if everything about you has changed.

It seems like you are living the life you were destined to live.

You are living the life you always dreamed of living. The life you knew was always possible for you.

A Moment of Reflection and Insight

As you reflect upon some of the wonderful and positive changes that have taken place in your life on this day, take out a piece of paper and write down the answers to the following questions:

1. Where are you living?
2. What are you doing that is so exciting and exhilarating?

3. Who are you with? What are they like?
4. What things do you have?
5. What do you look like?
6. How have you changed?
7. How do you feel?
8. How has your life changed for the better?

Now, review your answers and take away the insights you have gleaned from this exercise and write them down.

Going from Counsellor to Speaker

Sometime ago, I did this exercise and saw myself as a successful author and speaker.

I was living on a beautiful island. My book was a best seller, and I was in demand as a speaker. Everything in my imagination looked great.

Getting Real

I could have become overwhelmed and depressed since my dream life seemed so impossible to achieve. I also knew that it might take time to turn my dream into a reality. Somehow, I had to get started working toward my goal. I took immediate action and contacted the local newspaper and the local Toastmaster's Club.

If I was going to slowly move away from being a psychotherapist working in the field of psychiatry and move toward becoming an author and speaker, I had to somehow and in some way move toward the direction of my goal while supporting my family through my day job.

Bloom Where You are Planted...Do Some of Your Dream Even If You Can't Have It All Right Now

I did not start out writing a book. I contacted the local newspaper in town and asked them if I could write a weekly article called "Moments of Motivation". I knew the task of writing a book would be overwhelming to me; however, I started out small and did what I could with what I had and where I was, to get me headed in the direction I wanted to go. I must admit, the first few articles were poorly written, yet my writing skills improved over time. I also created quite a following of loyal readers who enjoyed the articles.

In terms of becoming a speaker, I knew I wasn't ready to keynote major conferences. I knew I had to improve my speaking skills and **do a part** of what I considered my big dream.

I joined Toastmaster's International and entered speaking competitions, winning several of them. My weekly articles that appeared in the local newspaper also resulted in invitations to speak at local clubs and schools.

I did not get paid for writing the articles and for most of the speaking engagements; however, I do believe that if you begin doing what you love to do, people will catch your energy and eventually the money will come.

Take Consistent Action Congruent with Your Dream

My advice is to dream big and start out small. Each week, I would see my articles being published in the newspaper. I clipped them and kept them in a folder. Each night before I went to bed, I would mentally and emotionally recall my victories of winning speaking contests. I would look at my trophies, ribbons, and certificates, and then repeat 'The Life You Always Dreamed of Living' exercise. My confidence, skills, and abilities were growing. I was making headway toward the fulfillment of my dream.

How?

By taking small steps on a consistent basis that were in line with my ultimate goal.

Translational Confidence

The experience I gained writing articles for the newspaper and magazine gave me the confidence to write this book.

I mean, if you can write several articles, then you can write several pages for a book, right?

Simply translating the confidence from small wins into pursuing bigger wins is really what it is all about.

What Can You Do?

After doing 'The Life You Have Always Dreamed of Living' exercise and discovering clearly what you want, ask yourself the following questions:

1. What can I do right now, even on a small scale, that will begin the process of moving me away from where I am and toward where I want to go?
2. If I could scale down my big dream and fit it into my life where I am right now, what could I do?
3. What small step could I take on a consistent basis that would take me in the direction I want to go?
4. What kind of person do I need to become in order to live out my dream? What changes can I make right now to begin making progress toward reaching that idea?
5. In what ways can I "bloom where I am planted"?
6. What can I begin doing now to get a few "small wins" under my belt in order to build and translate my confidence to take on an even bigger challenge?
7. Each morning write on a piece of paper the question, "What three things can I do today to become the type of person I want to become and create the type of life I want to live?" Make them small, achievable goals that will eventually take you in the direction you want to go in life.

Being clear about what you want and taking action on a consistent basis really proves to yourself and your brain that you truly mean business when it comes to changing yourself or the direction of your life.

Consider this acronym:

C - **Cut away** the confusion in terms of discovering the direction in your life by using 'The Life You Have Always Dreamed of Living' exercise.

L - **List** what you can do even on a small scale that is congruent with your ultimate goal.

A - **Accumulate** self-confidence by experiencing small wins and translating it toward setting and achieving more goals.

R - **Realize** that "anyone who is any good at anything needed a place to be bad." "Bloom where you are planted" and develop your skills.

I - **Instill** self-motivation by reviewing your wins and keep anything associated to your wins as reminders of your achievements.

T - **Take time** to repeat 'The Life You Have Always Dreamed of Living' exercise.

Y - **You are responsible** for taking daily action to create the life you want. Don't wait for others to motivate you.

Chapter 4

Keep It a Secret

"Loose lips sink ships." — Unknown

Once you have discovered how you want to change yourself or your life, keep it a secret! Don't tell anyone. Once you have reached a personal moment of breaking point, become clear about what it is you really want in your life, and have started to make small, consistent changes congruent with your ultimate goal, why do you think you need to tell everyone what you are doing?

You May Lose Your Day Job

Broadcasting your dream to others is one of the worst mistakes you can make.

Why?

Listen. I have been there. I'll tell you why.

Suppose you walk into work tomorrow and tell your co-workers that you have reached "breaking point". Suppose you tell them you are sick and tired of working for elephant's pay. Suppose you tell them that you have finally woken up, have smelled the coffee, and that in order to get ahead, you have chosen to become self-employed.

How do you think they will feel?

Do you think they will gather around the water cooler and cheer you on?

Do you think they will look for ways to support and help you?

Do you really think most of them really mean it when they say, "I'm happy for you. I think that is a great idea"?

Crabs in the Bucket

Apparently, I am told, that on certain beaches there are crabs children love to catch. I was told that if you place them in a wooden bucket they would all remain at the bottom simply circling each other. If one crab makes the effort to begin to climb up the side of the wooden bucket, another one or several will chase after it and seek to pull it back down to join the rest at the bottom.

Keep your dream a secret since the bottom dwellers in life, fueled by jealousy, may attempt to thwart your efforts to rise above them and escape the limitations of the circumstances and environment in which you co-exist.

The crabs in the bottom of the bucket have all kinds of ways to drain you of your mental and emotional energy. It seems as if some of them are emotional vampires that suck you dry and leave you with no energy left at the end of the day to pursue your goals to get ahead.

Let's Get Real

Chances are they will become jealous and envious. Why? Since you are working on changing yourself and your life, and they are still choosing to stay in their rut. They may even tell your boss that you have not been concentrating on doing your work during the day since you are starting your own business. They may look for ways to sabotage your day job, your credibility, or reputation just to complicate your life and slow you down in the process of achieving your dream.

People who do not have a dream for themselves usually cannot see it happening for anyone else and may seek to oppose them.

Let them waste their lunch hours talking about the outcomes on a television show contest. Let them complain about the government, management, and what should be done. Let them become engrossed in the petty problems and details of the lives of others.

Use your time and energy to create the life you have always dreamed of living and keep your progress a secret from those who live for the smaller things in life.

Family is Often the Worst

Don't broadcast your dreams to family either. They will usually remind you of all the other times you said you were going to change yourself or your life and failed. You don't need their criticism, ridicule, or rejection.

I recall a woman who wanted to lose weight and become fit. Whenever she attended family gatherings, she wore her old clothes that were baggy and made her look big.

Why?

In the past when she had worked on losing weight, her family would tell her that she was "getting too thin" and "wasting away". They would also pressure her to eat fattening foods. Certain family members became jealous that she might be making a positive change in her life. They feared she might "get ahead" of them somehow.

After she had lost her weight, improved her self-confidence, and made fitness a part of her lifestyle, they could no longer stop her from moving ahead despite their negative influence.

Jay Leno and His Mother's Response

Jay Leno, host of *The Tonight Show*, knew his mother wanted him in a career with more security. He would often call home and tell his mother about the wonderful opportunities available in the entertainment field.

Once he told his mother that Sylvester Stallone just made $12 million for ten weeks' work. His mother replied, "Yeah, but what happens those other forty-two weeks? What is he going to do if nothing else comes in?"

You Will Never Amount to Anything!

While in my teens just after my father passed away, I started attending a church in our area. The minister was an excellent speaker and his words and compassion brought comfort to me as a mixed-up, grieving young man.

I saw the powerful impact his messages had on myself and others and I thought, "That is what I want to do. I want to be able to help other people as he has helped me. I want to be a speaker and help people change their life!"

After a particular service, I was feeling great. I was thinking about becoming a speaker. I was dreaming about it. An elderly man came up to me and took me aside.

"How do you like our minister?" he asked.

"I think he's great. You know, one day I am going to speak to people just like he does. I am going to become a speaker and encourage and help people," I replied.

He took my arm and pulled me further away from the people walking out the door and said, "Listen. I know all about you. Your father is dead and you are a no-good punk. You play that rock music and have long hair. Listen. You will never become a speaker.

Who are you to think you could speak to doctors, lawyers, and educated people? Nobody would ever want to listen to you. You are no good and won't amount to anything in your life. You better get a job packing bags at the grocery store because that's all you will ever amount to!"

The pain of losing my father and the words of death this man spoke into my life at that time crushed my spirit. I broke down and cried as I quietly and anonymously left the church.

I have learned through the years that it is best to keep your dreams to yourself and then someday surprise your critics when you have reached your goals.

Don't broadcast your dreams until you get to the point where you are so far ahead, the critics can't catch up to you and pull you back.

Telling your dreams to others gives some nasty people the opportunity to crush them before their birth or as you develop them in their infancy stage.

De-Motivating Yourself

Sometimes I think that the more we keep talking about what we are going to do in our lives with others and broadcasting it all about actually can decrease our personal motivation level.

Why?

I think that part of us keeps on hearing with emotion what it is we intend to do and then when we do not take action toward the achieving what we have set out to do, part of the brain no longer believes what we say. I also think that when we broadcast our dreams to others they may wish us well with their words yet we may arouse feelings of jealousy and envy and may possibly evoke them to secretly or subconsciously curse our efforts.

Thoughts are energy and sometimes the negative thoughts of others directed toward us, in some mysterious way I believe, does have an impact on us and our lives. Wait until you are rounding third base before you give others any indication that you just hit a home run.

Tips for Keeping Your Dream a Secret

1. Don't tell anyone about your dream.
2. Make small changes on a consistent basis so small that people hardly even notice.
3. Operate in secrecy and in anonymity as best you can.
4. Try not to "up-play" any successes. Keep a low profile when you are around jealous and envious people who may try to create havoc in your life.

Do these until you have gained tremendous confidence; until you can manage criticism, ridicule, and rejection; until you know that, like a rocket, you are entering the unlimited territory of the universe and no one can stop you.

Then, have your "coming out" party and let all the bells in your belfry ring as loud as they can and refuse to let anyone stop you from moving even further ahead in your life.

S - **Seeking** to make a positive change often invites criticism, ridicule, or opposition.

E - **Engage** in making your dream a reality not an announcement.

C - **Cherish** your progress in your heart. Be careful not to reveal your heart desires to others.

R - **Revel** in your secret wins and personal victories.

E - **Engage** nosey people in a conversation about themselves, keeping the focus off of your progress toward your goals.

T - **Think** about your "coming out" party when you shock people with the successful accomplishment of your goal.

Chapter 5

Increase Your Energy Level

"I call energy the fuel of excellence. You can change your internal representations all day long, if your biochemistry is messed up, it's going to make the brain create distorted representations...It's highly unlikely you'll even feel like using what you've learned." — Anthony Robbins

Unless you want to become a professional couch potato, making any type of positive change in your life will probably require you to increase your physical, mental, and emotional energy levels.

The Daily Grind

Once you have come to the place of breaking point, know exactly what you want, and have kept it a secret, it is important to take your dream beyond something that exists as a little "home movie" your head.

Now comes the time when you must choose to blow past the trap of the exhausting daily grind in order to blast yourself away from where you are to get to where you want to go.

This requires increasing your energy level.

I'm Too Tired

The daily grind will give you a million and one excuses to quit. The best one most people use is, **"I can't do it right now. I am too tired. I will do it tomorrow."**

In my seminars, I teach people a very powerful technique they can use to easily overcome procrastination and take action. If you only have enough energy to make it through the work day, come home, have supper, watch television for a few hours, and then crawl into the sack, you probably won't reach your goals.

Why?

Achieving any goal will most likely require you to have more physical, mental, and emotional energy than just making it through the day.

Winners wake up early and sometimes work late.

Winners know that they must invest in keeping their energy levels up.

Winners treat their bodies like a high performance machine and fuel it with the right foods and liquids to get optimum results.

Selling Out to Simple Pleasures

Those who are trapped in the daily grind and who fail to increase their energy level may seek to find small panaceas to break the pace of their boring, predictable lives.

Some spend money they don't have. Some find the highlight of their week is dining at an "all you can eat" buffet. Some are addicted to certain television shows. Some become entangled in the tiny details of the lives of others.

It is easier to buy into the 'Simple Pleasures' theory of life. The 'Simple Pleasures' theory is accepting your life as it is, looking forward to your double double coffee in the morning, and your annual trip to the all-inclusive resort in a tropical paradise once a year. This is easier than making changes in your life in order to live out your destiny, access more of your God-given potential, and become the best you really can be.

Practical Ways to Increase Your Physical Energy

Make sure you consult with your family doctor before you begin any exercise program or consider taking any health food products, vitamins, or supplements.

Join a Gym

Get a personal trainer at the local gym to set you up with a program to slowly get yourself in shape. Being fit is one way to increase your physical energy.

Hire a Personal Trainer to Come to Your Home

Isn't it amazing how we will spend money on an expensive, high fat meal, using a spoon to dig ourselves into an early grave, and yet we are reluctant to spend the same amount of money for advice on how to get fit, create more physical energy, improve our mood, and potentially live longer?

We will spend money to keep our ducts clean, to buy additives to clean our fuel injection systems in our cars, to watch a play, or attend a sporting event. However, for approximately the same price, we can have a professional come into our home and coach us to better health that will improve our energy level.

Make the Local Health Food Store Your Favourite Place to Shop

Grab all the free magazines they have to offer. Borrow books from their library if they have one. Hang out in the store with the health enthusiasts and learn what makes them tick. Discover how to fuel the vehicle which will take you from where you are now in your life to where you want to go.

Make Small Changes in What You Eat and Drink

Exchange cups of coffee for pure, filtered water. Give up processed foods for protein shakes, organic beans, plain oatmeal, and healthy products. Eat nutritious power bars from the health food store instead of chocolate bars.

Some fitness experts advise eating six small meals the size of the palm of your hand, with a combination of one protein and one carbohydrate.[4] This will keep your metabolic system revved up to give you energy, burn fat, and help you over the mid-afternoon slump.

One of my favourites is eating a banana with a couple spoonfuls of all natural peanut butter. People think I am weird. Everywhere I go I carry a small black bag with bottled water and greens powder in a container. If I am in a meeting, taking a break during a seminar, or traveling, I often take out my shaker cup, dump in some greens powder, pour in some water, shake it up and drink it. People ask me, "What's that?" "Fuel for my body to keep me going," I reply. One time I was transferred to a different office and my new co-worker said, "I guess I have to work with a guy who drinks his lunch out of a cup." I thought it was kind of cool that word had spread about my unusual nutrition habit.

Grow in Knowledge

Learn as much as you can about what is best for your health and your body. Your nutrition and fitness level affects the amount of physical energy you will have. Learn how to maintain and fuel your body in the same way an owner of a formula one class racing car would take care of their precious high-performance vehicle.

Increasing Your Mental and Emotional Energy

Whiners at Work

Try to avoid those at work who always seem to be complaining about everyone and everything. Ask them, "What do you think would be a solution to this?"

They will often quit complaining to you since you are leading them into a constructive thinking mode.

'Molehills into Mountain People' at Work

These people will exhaust your mental and emotional energy by taking a small situation (which they call an "incident") and turning it into a major catastrophe or crisis.

I am amazed at how many supervisors and managers have little insight into the fact that these "Molehill into Mountain" people are usually the ones who talk a good game and yet often in reality do very little.

Be careful you do not get emotionally drawn into their latest drama, using up your emotional energy by allowing yourself to synchronize emotionally with them over minor issues that they have transformed into major events.

Once these type of people get a whiff that you are working toward improving yourself, your life, or finding a way out of a negative toxic work environment, they often work all that much harder to embroil you in petty workplace conflicts that will suck the energy out of you.

Effectively Manage Criticism and Negativity

When somebody criticizes you, it can drain your physical, mental, and emotional energy as you attempt to defend yourself or argue your point. Save your energy and learn to respond to them by saying, "Perhaps you're right." Then, lead them into giving you a suggestion.

'Perhaps You're Right' Example

Suppose somebody came up to me after a talk and said, "You are the worst speaker I have ever heard. Coming here tonight was a complete waste of my time."

Using the 'Perhaps You're Right' technique, I would respond by saying, "Perhaps you're right. Perhaps I am the worst speaker you have ever heard. Perhaps this was a waste of your time. I was wondering if you could give me some tips on how I might improve my speaking skills and bring more value to the hour?"

You are not agreeing with the person in totality. You are agreeing in probability by using this technique.

People always ask me how they can deal with the criticism and negativity of the person they 'have to live with'. Use this technique to disarm them, put them in a solution-focused mode, and protect your self-esteem.

Increasing your level of physical, mental, and emotional energy is key to making consistent progress toward the achievement of your goal.

Key Points to Remember When it Comes to Increasing Your Energy Level

E - **Eat** nutritious foods and drink pure water.

N - **Notice** who it is in your life that drains your mental and emotional energy.

E - **Ensure** that you are not sucked into the emotional vortex of others and being drained of your own energy. Tell yourself, "If I buy into their insanity and vanity, I will be robbing myself of energy I need to accomplish my goals."

R - **Respond** to criticism and negativity by using the 'Perhaps You're Right' technique.

G - **Get out** of the lunchroom or staffroom and get around positive people.

Y - **You must learn** to identify and detach yourself from the emotional vampires that will sink their teeth into you and suck you dry, leaving you very little physical, emotional, and mental energy left to focus on achieving your goals.

Chapter 6

Consult a Successful Role Model

ℭ

"He who can copy, can do." – Leonardo DaVinci

Whatever it is you want to achieve in your life, there is someone else in the same place you are right now who has already achieved the goal you want to achieve. Why not learn from them?

The Minefield Experiment

Suppose you wanted to cross a minefield and you saw a set of footprints in the dirt from a person who had already successfully made it to the other side.

What would you do?

Would you just walk through the minefield and cut your own path? Or would you follow in the footsteps of the person who had already successfully made it across and left footprints behind for you to follow?

It makes sense for us to consult with and follow a successful role model before we begin making major changes in our lives.

The Master Painter

I once was in the painting business and competed against painters who were charging $30.00 per room with the customer supplying the paint. It was tough to make a buck.

I noticed this older gentleman at the paint store who never seemed in a hurry, drove a nice van, and who always seemed to have lots of cash on him. I knew there had to be a strategy to his success.

One day he asked me if I wanted to help him on a job and he would pay me by the hour. I agreed. We drove in his van to one of the richest neighborhoods in the city. We got out, and he rang the door bell at a beautiful, luxurious home. The woman greeted us and invited us in. He then removed his shoes and put on a brand new pair of slippers and handed me a pair to do the same.

"I always use a new pair of slippers at every job. I don't want germs from the outside coming into your home off my shoes," he said to the customer.

The guy was a real pro. Let's face it; he was a class act. He never gave estimates; he only left an invoice. He turned certain people down since their home wasn't "worthy" of his work. He finished each job one at a time. He used only top quality materials. He always had on a clean white shirt and white pants when he worked in someone's home. He would repaint for free if he thought a finished job was still "unacceptable" to him. He would put on quite a show and charge piles of money. He made the customers beg him to come and paint in their home. He would tell people, "Three months. Three months from now is the earliest I could possibly even consider viewing your home before considering doing any work in it." Customers loved to brag to others in the upscale neighborhood how they had this "wonderful man" come and "beautify" their home with painting and decorating expertise from a "master".

He was an "artist and craftsman". If you referred to him as a common painter you would insult him and place him in the ranks of the common riff raff who slosh paint on walls rather than create a new "exquisite atmosphere".

It wasn't long before I realized that it's **"the sizzle that sells the steak"**.

I followed his same practices but just put my own unique spin on them and had more free time, made more money, and had people calling me to paint in their elegant and beautiful homes. I went from making $30 per room to charging, in some cases, $300.00 per room.

How? By following a successful role model.

How to Find a Successful Role Model

You can find a successful role model by hanging out in places where they exist.

For example, when I wanted to learn about weight lifting and getting fit, I talked to people in the gym who knew all the tricks connected to eating right and exercising the right way to achieve results. I didn't consult the overweight guy walking on the treadmill in his basement with a bag of chips in his hand and an ashtray welded to the frame.

When I wanted to learn how to play rock music on the guitar, I went for one guitar lesson to a lady who wanted to teach me how to pick out "Mary had a Little Lamb". "Enough of that!" I said to myself. I went to a music store filled with guys my age who could play the rock songs I wanted to learn. If they sounded just like the tunes on the LP (Oops! I think I am revealing insights into my age here.) I would invite them back to my house, give them ten bucks, five or six hotdogs, and ask them to show me how they played those songs.

You can find a successful role model by reading an autobiography of someone who has accomplished what you want to achieve.

You can find a successful role model by writing to them and asking them for advice.

You can examine anyone who is already successful at whatever it is you want to accomplish and analyze their strategy connected to how they got there.

Hockey's Masked Men

When our son, Alexander, had an interest in goaltending, he studied some of the great goalies by watching the hockey games on television.

We picked him up a video called *Hockey's Masked Men*. It explained the different styles of goaltending used by some of the top goalies in the world.

Alex watched the video over and over and began to practice the different goaltending moves while playing ball hockey in our driveway.

After work one day, I arrived at the arena to see the most amazing goaltending for a boy his age. After his game, people congratulated him and commented on his extraordinary abilities.

"Dad, Dad! Did you see me play? I used all the tricks I learned off of the video tape and combined them all into my own style!" he blurted out.

Alex had learned from the masters. He had learned how to combine the best of the best and injected his own unique style into the process. He created a hybrid approach to goaltending, achieving outstanding unique results.

Now he is interested in guitar. It isn't very quiet around our house anymore with the sounds of different rock stars being cranked out from his amp in the basement below.

Milton Erikson said, "We can pretend anything and master it." Start acting "as if" you were your role model. How do they move? How do they think? How do they speak? What do they believe? What are their finger prints of excellence?

Inject Your Own Style...Be Yourself!

Find and use a successful role model. Learn some of their basic and advanced strategies. Remember that you are unique and don't overlook your own strengths and abilities.

Successful role models can often show you the footprints that will take you from where you are now to where you want to go.

Whether you are determined and disciplined enough to take the steps to cross over to the other side and what you do once you get there is completely up to you.

The Retired Consultant

Harry, a millwright, had been offered a package for over 20 years of service and was let go from the company. He was replaced by a much younger man with far more credentials.

One of the machines on the production line began to make a terrible noise and failed to work. The crew worked on it for days; yet, they were unable to get it functioning.

"Let's call in old Harry. Nobody knows this machine like he does," said the plant manager.

Harry came in and listened to the machine for a few minutes. He then picked up a hammer and whacked the side of the machine in a particular spot. The machine started working immediately. "Send us a bill, Harry. I guess we could call you a consultant now," said the plant manager.

A few days later, the plant manager received a call from the accounting department and was asked to explain the invoice Harry submitted. Harry had invoiced the company for the amount of $3,003.00 for his consulting services.

The plant manager sent an email to Harry asking him to itemize his charges. Everyone thought this was a ridiculous amount to bill the company when Harry had only been there less than ten minutes.

Harry sent them his itemized invoice which read:

Hitting the machine with a hammer......*$3.00*
Knowing where to hit it.................*$3,000.00*

No matter what it is you want to accomplish in your life, consult a successful role model who has already been where you want to go, who has achieved what you aspire to achieve, and who knows the right places to strike to produce specific outcomes.

Use the W.I.N. Approach to Role Modeling Your Way to Success

W - **Watch** and learn from those who are achieving the outcomes in their life that you desire to experience.

I - **Imitate** what they do and how they do it. Start doing what they are doing to get the results they are getting.

N - **Notice** how you can develop your own unique style. Learn the basics from the masters and create your hybrid approach, injecting your own unique personality, skills, and abilities.

Chapter 7

See Yourself Succeeding at Whatever it is You Want to Accomplish Before it Even Takes Place

℘

"Your imagination is a preview of life's coming attractions." – Albert Einstein

The birthplace of any and all achievement begins within our own mind.

Breaking point takes place as you think about all the pain and frustration you have and will experience in your life if you do not change.

Discovering how you would like your life to be different begins by looking within and seeing how your life could be so much better. It is getting clear about the specific outcomes and results you want to achieve. It is about designing your future self and life.

Seeing yourself succeed before it even takes place draws you toward the achievement of your goal. It motivates you to be persistent in taking daily action to achieve your goals. It plays a mysterious role in drawing to you the resources and opportunities you need to shape your life into that which you have envisioned. It involves playing your own mental movie in the theatre of your own mind, written by, directed by, and starring you in the lead role.

How Does 'Seeing Yourself Succeed Before It Even Takes Place' Thinking Work?

First, you picture in your mind what it is you want to have, do, or become. This sets your subconscious mind in motion in terms of activating your sensory acuity. Sensory acuity means that you will subconsciously always be on the lookout for opportunities, people, and resources you will require in order for you to experience whatever it is you have pictured in your mind.

When we visualize, our subconscious mind draws us in the direction toward what we imagine. Our emotions become stirred as we contemplate all of the feelings we anticipate experiencing as we move toward achieving our goal. Our will is engaged and influences us to make decisions and choices that are congruent with the mental picture of whatever it is we desire to achieve. Our body then acts and reacts as we take physical action to produce a change in our circumstances to alter them to align with our vision.

Let me get real with you.

When I think about a large chocolate milkshake, see it in my mind, feel the texture of the cold milk and ice cream mixed together, and remember experiencing the taste of the chocolate, my subconscious mind is not looking for the nearest health food store to buy a power bar!

All the bells are ringing, and I am subconsciously sharpening my senses to alert me to any signs of a place where I can buy a chocolate milkshake.

My mental picture of what I want influences my desires. My desires influence my will. My will directs my behavior, and so I look for whatever it is that will meet my desires. I then exercise my will to choose and then take action.

I also experience the rewards or consequences of my actions.

Secondly, when you picture something in your mind and imagine whatever it is you want to do, have, or become, you send out vibrational energy simply by using your thoughts.

Our thoughts are energy. By our thoughts, we send out signals that attract into our lives whatever it is we consistently picture in our mind.

I recall reading about an experiment in which two plants were grown under ideal conditions. As they were in the process of growing, pictures of them were taken and given to two groups of people. The picture of the one plant was given to a group of people who merely thought such things as, "I hate you. You will never grow. You are ugly." The picture of the other plant was given to a group of people who looked at the photograph and projected thoughts such as, "You are beautiful. You will grow tall and strong. You are lovely and beautiful."

The first plant with the negative thoughts projected on it failed to grow and shriveled up. The other plant with positive thoughts directed toward it flourished. This happened even though the plants grew under the same conditions and were thousands of miles away from both groups who were projecting their mental energy to them by staring at a photograph.

The Power of Thoughts and Words

Dr. Joseph Murphy in *The Power of Your Subconscious Mind* relates a story which illustrates the power of our thoughts and words to shape the outcomes we experience in our lives.

He writes:

"For many years I gave a regular series of lectures at the London Truth Forum in Caxton Hall, which I founded a number of years ago. Dr. Evelyn Fleet, the director, told me about a man whose young daughter suffered from both crippling rheumatoid arthritis and the disfiguring and painful skin condition called psoriasis. They tried many treatments, but nothing the doctors did seemed to help. The man was near despair. Over and over he said, to himself and to his friends, 'I would give my right arm to see my daughter cured.'

According to Dr. Fleet, one day the family was out for a drive. Their car was involved in a head-on collision. The father's right arm was torn off at the shoulder. When he came home from the hospital, he discovered that his daughter's arthritis and skin condition had vanished."[5]

Successful People Who have Used the Mental Imagery Technique

After retiring from body building, Arnold Schwarzenegger was asked by an interviewer, "What are you going to do next?"

"I am going to become the number one box office star in all of Hollywood," replied Arnold.

The interviewer was skeptical, given Arnold's previous film work, his body size, and his thick Austrian accent.

"How are you going to do that?" the interviewer asked.

"It's the same process I used in body building. What you do is create a vision of who you want to be and then live into that picture as if it were already true," Arnold explained.

Arnold did move on to achieving his dream.

Jim Carrey's Secret

In 1990, Jim Carrey, then an unknown comic, wrote a cheque to himself for the amount of 10 million dollars for "Acting Services Rendered". The cheque was post-dated Thanksgiving 1995.

He earned about $800,000 for his work in the movies *Ace Ventura* and *The Mask*. Then, in 1994, he was paid $7 million for his role in *Dumb and Dumber*. In 1995, he earned many more millions and achieved his envisioned goal.

Celine Dion's Childhood Vision

Singer, Celine Dion, was asked if she ever thought that she would sell millions of records and perform singing tours in front of thousands of people each week. She said that none of this had surprised her. She had imagined all of it happening ever since she was five years old.

Getting In Shape with a Picture

One young woman who was severely overweight had tried everything to lose it and get into shape. However, she kept relapsing back into her old habits. Her mother took a picture of her and cut her head out of it. She then glued the picture of the young woman's head to a picture of a lean, fit body taken from the swimwear section of a summer catalog. She then posted this picture on the fridge door with a magnet. The young woman, struggling with her weight issues, would see what she "could become" each time she went to open the fridge door. She was successful in matching the body image posted on the fridge door since she began to make healthier food choices each time she went into the fridge for something to eat.

Improving Sports Performance

Sports psychologist, Lars Erik Unastal, examined how the top downhill skiers improved their techniques and their odds of winning skiing competitions. He discovered that the top performers mentally rehearsed their run over and over in the theater of their own minds.

Walt Disney Seeing His Dream Come True

Apparently, upon the construction of Disney World, two of the main engineers responsible for its completion stood together and looked over their finished work.

"It's too bad Walt wasn't here to see all of this," the one engineer said to the other.

"He did see it—long before it was ever built," replied the other engineer.

Scott Adams and 'Dilbert'

Scott Adams dreamed of being a famous cartoonist while he was working at a utility company. According to Laurence Boldt, Scott read in an article in *Newsweek Magazine* that, "The basic idea is that fifteen times a day you write down whatever it is your goal is. Then you'll observe things happening that will make that objective more likely to happen. It's actually a process of forcing your environment to change."[6]

He wrote down fifteen times a day, "I will become a syndicated cartoonist."

Today, he is a popular cartoonist with his work in syndication.

See your goal and affirm your goal by writing out exactly what it is you want to achieve.

The Man Who Walked Into Freedom

Dr. Lothar von Blenk-Schmidt was held captive in a Soviet prison camp during World War II. He saw beyond his current circumstances and by using mental imagery was able to set himself free. Here is his account:

"I was a prisoner of war in a coal mine in Russia, and I saw men dying all around me in that prison compound. We were watched over by brutal guards, arrogant officers, and sharp, fast-thinking commissars. After a short medical checkup, a quota of coal was assigned to each person. My quota was three hundred pounds per day. In case any man did not fill his quota, his small food ration was cut down, and in a short time he was resting in the cemetery.

I started concentrating on my escape. I knew that my subconscious mind would somehow find a way. My home in Germany was destroyed, my family wiped out; all my friends and former associates were either killed in the war or were in concentration camps.

I said to my subconscious mind, 'I want to go to Los Angeles, and you will find the way.' I had seen pictures of Los Angeles and I remembered some of the boulevards very well as well as some of the buildings.

Every day and night I would imagine I was walking down Wilshire Boulevard with an American girl whom I met in Berlin prior to the war (she is now my wife). In my imagination we would visit the stores, ride buses, and eat in the restaurants. Every night I made it a special point to drive my imaginary American automobile up and down the boulevards of Los Angeles. I made all this vivid and real. These pictures in my mind were as real and as natural to me as one of the trees outside the prison camp.

Every morning the chief guard would count the prisoners as they were lined up. He would call out "one, two, three," etc., and when seventeen was called out, which was my number in sequence, I stepped aside. In the meantime, the guard was called away for a minute or so, and on his return he started by mistake on the next man as number seventeen. When the crew returned in the evening, the number of men was the same, and I was not missed, and the discovery would take a long time.

I walked out of the camp undetected and kept walking for twenty-four hours, resting in a deserted town the next day. I was able to live by fishing and killing some wildlife. I found coal trains going to Poland and traveled on them by night, until finally I reached Poland. With the help of friends, I made my way to Lucerne, Switzerland.

One evening at the Palace Hotel, Lucerne, I had a talk with a man and his wife from the United States of America. This man asked me if I would care to be a guest at his home in Santa Monica, California. I accepted, and when I arrived in Los Angeles, I found that their chauffeur drove me along Wilshire Boulevard and many other boulevards which I had imagined so vividly in the long months in the Russian coal mines. I recognized the buildings which I had seen in my mind so often. It actually seemed as if I had been in Los Angeles before. I had reached my goal.

I will never cease to marvel at the wonders of the subconscious mind. Truly, it has ways we know not of."[7]

I Was Here Long Before You Invited Me to Come

My wife and I drove by this beautiful resort, and I blurted out, "I want to speak there, make a bunch of money, and pay off our credit line."

I pulled over and went into the resort. I then went to the front desk and asked the clerk to show me the biggest conference room available.

"Are you planning to hold a meeting or conference, sir?" he asked.

"No. However, I do plan on attending one in this room and speaking here," I replied.

"On what date, sir?" he asked.

"I'm not sure yet, but a final date will shape up for me," I replied.

I walked up to the podium and imagined speaking to a group of people from a corporation. As I imagined this, I gripped the podium with both of my hands.

I imagined a corporation phoning me up and asking me to come to this very resort to speak to a group of sales representatives. I imagined myself telling them the fee I charged, and when the person would hesitate, I would say with boldness, "I am worth it!" I imagined typing up the invoice and later going to the mailbox to pick up my cheque.

"Thanks for showing me the room. I will see you again," I said to the clerk as I left.

I kept seeing in my mind all the things I believed would happen and expected to happen.

The Phone Call

It was early on a Saturday morning that a corporation contacted me about speaking to their group of sales representatives.

"I suppose you are holding it at such and such a resort," I said.

"Yes, how did you know?" the person replied.

"I'll bet it is being held in the Acorn Room. Am I correct?" I asked.

"Yes, but how did you know?" the person questioned.

I was then asked what I charged and told the person the amount I wanted.

"You are not cheap. That seems like a lot of money," they replied.

"I'm worth it!" boldly came my reply.

"It sure sounds like you are. We will pay your fee," the person replied.

The person booking me for the date went on to say how they just couldn't figure out why they felt compelled to book me, a "no namer," when they had a budget to book a big name speaker.

Afterwards, a staff member came up to me and said, "How in the world did an unknown guy like you get to speak at our event?"

I looked them straight in the eye and said, "They had no choice but to book me to speak here today. You see, I was here before the event was even planned by your company."

How to Use Mental Imagery to Achieve Your Goals

1. Develop a clear mental picture of who you would like to become, what you would like to have, or what you want to accomplish in your life. Some people find it helpful to create a scrapebook with pictures cut from magazines to help them focus their mind on what they want.

2. Find a quiet, comfortable place. Imagine seeing yourself already succeeding at whatever it is you want to become, have, or do. First, see yourself as if you were on a movie screen. Notice any colors, sounds, feelings, smells, and tastes connected to the images. Then see yourself actually entering the movie and experiencing the feelings connected to the events.

3. Rehearse this daily and make the feelings connected to you living out what you see even more intense — as if you have already accomplished your goal.

4. Prepare in advance and in "faith" in some ways for the day when you will actually experience what you want to take place. For example, if you want to own a BMW, buy a BMW key chain and carry your existing car keys on it. If you want to lose weight, buy a pair of jeans the size you envision yourself wearing and keep them in a place in your closet where you can see them each morning as you pick out the clothes you plan to wear each day.

5. Refuse to think about your current circumstances. Use mental imagery to take you where you want to be in your life, not where you want to stay. Do not focus on your limitations, your past, or your current circumstances. Move beyond your self-scripted limitations and focus on seeing a new and different future for yourself.

Use the S.E.E. Approach to Achieving Your Goals

S - Spend time in the theater of your own mind seeing yourself having, becoming, or doing whatever it is you want.

E - Engage in using all your senses when seeing yourself succeed. What will it look like? How will you feel? What will you hear yourself saying? What smells or tastes might be connected to what you see?

E - **Energize** your mental images by preparing in advance by faith before they arrive. For example, start building your new wardrobe for the position you expect to be in one day.

Chapter 8

Create a Personal Plan of Action

❦

"First say to yourself what you would be; then do what you have to do." – Epictetus

You and I can come to the place of breaking point. We can be clear and focused in terms of what we want in our life. We can keep our dream a secret to minimize resistance and opposition. We can increase our physical and mental energy levels to improve our current physical, emotional, and psychological state. We can consult a successful role model and learn from their experience. We can also see ourselves succeeding at whatever it is we want to accomplish before it even takes place.

However, we will experience frustration, depression, and self-delusion if we fail to develop a strategy and take action toward the accomplishment of our goals.

Someone once said, "If you fail to plan, you plan to fail."

My Modeling Career

I remember as a boy seeing the picture of an airplane on a box in a hobby store that captivated my attention. It was a scale model assembled, painted, and decaled.

In putting together my first model, I quickly peeled off the cellophane wrapping and removed the lid from the box. I thought, "Man, all I have to do is look at the colored picture on the box, stick this thing together, slap some paint on it, and it will look exactly like the cool plane on the front of the box."

I soon realized that building a model airplane from a kit involved more than I had simply imagined.

First, the picture of the finished product motivated me to begin the process of building the plane. Secondly, the model came with a blueprint and specific steps to be followed on how to build the thing. Thirdly, there was the extra cost of the glue, brushes, and various small bottles of paint. Fourthly, it required patience to wait for one piece of the model to dry before proceeding with the next step.

These are the similar steps you and I need to follow once we have a picture of what we want to achieve in our lives. We need more than just a picture. We need to develop a blueprint—a step-by-step plan—that will move us away from where we are now to where we want to go in our lives.

How can we do that?

Create our own personal plan of action.

Creating Your Personal Plan of Action

Once you have decided exactly what it is you want to achieve and the outcomes you want to see take place in your life, follow these nine principles for creating a personal strategy.

1. Know Exactly What the Outcomes are that You Want to Achieve

Make sure you have a clear mental picture of what it is you want to accomplish. Write down what it is you want to have, do, or become in a journal and review it daily.

2. Define the Resources You Will Require

Brainstorm and jot down a list of everything you think you might need in order to get you from where you are now to where you want to go. Sometimes people spend more time and energy deciding and organizing all the resources they need for a camping trip or their funeral than they do in planning to change their life or achieve their goals.

3. Count the Cost

What is it going to cost you to achieve your goal?

What are you willing to sacrifice?

What might others have to sacrifice?

What will it cost you in terms of a commitment in time, money, and energy?

What will it cost you in terms of your relationships with others?

Bunker Hunt, the Texas oil billionaire, was asked, "What does it take to be a success?" He said that being successful is simple. "First, you decide what you want specifically; and second, you decide if you are willing to pay the price to make it happen—and then pay that price. If you don't take the second step, you'll never have what you want."

Yvon Chouinard believed he could create a better ice ax for himself and other ice climbers. He did develop the perfect ice ax. However, he started out selling them from the trunk of his car while living off of wild game he hunted in the forests on his travels and on cat food he bought by the case. He now has a 50 million dollar business selling specialized ice climbing equipment throughout the world.

4. Make a List of Mini-Goals

Take out a blank sheet of paper and write down your main goal in the centre of the page.

Then draw small circles around the main goal in the centre of the page. Inside each of these small circles write in the mini-goals that must be accomplished that will lead you to the eventual achievement of your main goal.

Once you have all your mini-goals written in the small circles surrounding your main goal, prioritize them. Put them in order to develop a game plan for yourself.

5. Set Some Time Frames

When setting your main goal and your mini-goals, decide on a deadline as to when you want to have them accomplished. If you aim for nothing, you will probably hit nothing.

6. Seek Professional Advice

Get professional advice or hire a professional to do what is not in your skill set. Sometimes we spend hours attempting to work on something connected to the achievement of our goal which a professional with the proper training and resources can do in minutes.

7. Take the First Step

Take action and begin working on completing your first mini-goal. Then, inspect what you expect in order to see if you are getting the results you had planned to achieve.

8. Make Plans to Reward Yourself

After completing a few mini-goals and especially after completing your main goal, have a reward set up for yourself and possibly others to enjoy.

9. Inspect What You Expect

Monitor your progress and outcomes to see if you are achieving the results you expected and if you are hitting the targets you are aiming for. If not, then change your strategy.

Beware of Paralysis of Analysis

Sometimes we can become consumed in the planning process. We can enjoy it more than taking action and making progress.

During Stonewall Jackson's valley campaign, his army was on one side of the river when it needed to be on the other side. Jackson told his engineers to plan and build a bridge in order for the army to cross. He also told the wagon master that is was crucial that they get to the other side as soon as possible.

The wagon master and his crew gathered all the logs, rocks, and fence rails they could find and built a bridge.

The next morning, General Jackson was told by the wagon master that all the supplies and artillery had crossed the river.

"Where are the engineers? What are they doing?" General Jackson asked.

"They are in their tent drawing up plans to build a bridge," the wagon master replied.

Be careful you do not sabotage yourself by focusing all your time on developing a strategy to achieve your goals and remain stuck in this phase, using it as a subconscious excuse to procrastinate.

Someone once said, "Plan the work and then work the plan!"

Beware of the Gadget Syndrome

The gadget syndrome happens when people set a goal for themselves and become more excited about purchasing all the gadgets they will need to accomplish their goal rather than focusing on taking action to achieve the goal itself.

For example, a person who desires to become an accomplished artist spends thousands of dollars purchasing all the top line supplies they believe they need and build an art studio onto their existing home. Once they have all they need to begin painting, they fail to get started since they need more tools, etc. They never really begin painting anything since they are consumed with buying things they believe they need to have before they begin. In the end, most of these folks simply never follow through, and wind up selling all their expensive gadgets at a fraction of the purchase price.

A Summary of How to Create Your Personal Plan of Action

P - Pinpoint the outcomes that you want to achieve.

L - List the resources you will need to accomplish your objective.

A - Accomplish mini-goals that will eventually take you to the place of achieving your ultimate goal.

N - Notice if you are getting the outcomes and results you want. If not, consider changing your approach or seek to learn from a successful role model.

Chapter 9

How to Effectively Manage Setbacks, Sabotage, and Disappointment

ℭ

"Show me someone who has done something worthwhile, and I'll show you someone who has overcome adversity." – Lou Holtz

There is a story about a chicken and a pig who were walking along the street together. The chicken saw a sign in a restaurant window that read, "Breakfast Special. Bacon and eggs - $1.99."

The chicken turned to the pig and said, "Mr. Pig, how about we go in there and have ourselves that breakfast special?"

The pig turned to the chicken and said, "That's easy for you to say. All that is required of you is a donation, but for me this means full commitment."

Staying Committed in Tough Times

It seems like the moment you begin to make any type of positive change in your life that some kind of resistance, opposition, or setback takes place. This is the point at which most people give up. In fact, 90% of those who begin any kind of self-improvement program will fail.

Why?

Most of us have never been taught how to handle the hurts, the failure, and the setbacks we often encounter while working toward the accomplishment of our dream.

Sometimes I think it seems as if life tests us over and over again to see if we really do have the heart to stick it out.

The Crash

In 1995, I was in a serious car accident that left me with "limitations" as I was told. The professionals called them "limitations". I called them—"My back is wrecked, and I'm dragging my left leg. I stutter, and I can't remember anything. I'm out of the game of life."

I was really in a bad way. I remember going to the specialist and enduring a four hour assessment and examination. In the end, he tells me, "You will go from a cane to a walker to a wheelchair. There is nothing we can do for you. I will fill out the disability papers for you right now."

I broke down and cried.

Here I was—a speaker who stuttered, who had no short term memory as a result of having my head whacked on the windshield, and who was in severe pain all the time; and there was nothing they could do for me.

There was talk of rehabilitation. "What's there to rehabilitate? I'm done," I said to myself.

Pills and Spills

I was on different medications and barely knew what day it was most of the time. Once I drove into town and forgot why I was there. I went to a payphone to call home and ask why I was in town. When I went to dial my number, I couldn't remember it! I was so frustrated and felt so helpless. I had to call for operator assistance to ask for my own phone number! Standing in the phone booth as people passed by on the street, I cried tears mixed with frustration, pain, and a sense of hopelessness.

I have great compassion for people who are in physical pain and whose lives have been radically altered by an accident of some kind. I know what it's like to be seen as a "whiner and a faker". I know how people look at you and what they say behind your back. I know how it affects your family and your relationships with others. I know how you want to talk about how much pain you are in, and how most people could care less. It can be a real lonely place in your life.

The End of My Dream

I was depressed and had all the medications to prove it. I would spend hours sorting out nuts and bolts in the basement. I thought I was down there for twenty minutes; however, my wife told me I had been down there for a lot longer.

Was this what my life was reduced to in order to gain some sense of achievement and self-esteem?

The insurance company covered the loss of income from all the speaking engagements I had already booked and been contracted to fulfill.

Free money—who cares!

I wanted my life back.

I was in so much pain I couldn't play ball hockey with my kids, go for hikes, biking, or make love with my wife. I prayed and asked God to heal me. It seemed that even He had dropped off the radar screen of my life. Where was He when I needed Him the most? Where was He when life came down to the crunch?

One afternoon while laying in bed in severe pain, feeling hopeless and whacked out on different medications, the thought enter my head that it would be better off if I were dead. The more I tried to get that thought out of my head, the more it persisted.

I thought about how I would do it. I believed everyone would be better off without having me around since I was such a burden. I kept my thoughts to myself and had planned to make preparations the next morning to follow through with my intentions.

Hey. Listen to me, please. If you ever find your-self in this place, don't be stupid like I was. Call for professional help. See your doctor right away! Get to the emergency department of the nearest hospital. Call a crisis line!

The next morning I woke up thinking about what all the experts had told me about my condi-tion, and how there was nothing they could do for me. I thought of my kids not having a dad who could play with them. I thought of the specialist who began filling out my disability papers right in front of me. I remembered seeing people in the rehabilitation part of the building being cheered on by a therapist as they pulled a cable on an exercise machine. I thought of why I was born. I knew it was to inspire others to achieve their dreams. How could I help others achieve their dreams when it seemed as if all of mine were gone?

I knew I had to make a choice at this point in my life. It was a turning point. Hey, the strange thing about turning points is that sometimes life takes you to the edge and being there is a very scary place.

I played all the scenes through my mind over and over again. I guess I just couldn't get that scene out of my head when the specialist told me things are going to go from bad to worse.

I could feel the intensity building within. My feelings of depression turned to intense anger. "Who are they to tell me what the outcome of my life will be?"

"Who are they to say, 'I'm all washed up'?"

"If I can't have my old life back, then I will make the best of what I have left!"

"God, give me the strength and wisdom to turn this all around," I said within myself.

I hauled my sorry butt out of bed and started scrounging around for my jogging shoes and track suit. Prior to my accident, I was jogging 45 minutes a day.

"Where are you going?" asked my wife.

"I'm tired of living like this. I am going for a walk. I am going to get my life back!" I said.

Please do not attempt to do such a thing unless you seek medical advice. I am telling you my story and not advising you to do the same.

I went out into the cold and began walking in the snow. "Just ten minutes. That's all. Just ten minutes for today. Five minutes one way and five minutes back home. You can do it! God, give me the strength for ten minutes!" I said to myself.

Five minutes down the road, I turned and looked back. I saw one footprint in the snow and a path left from the injured leg that dragged along behind me.

I looked at my leg that kept me immobilized and spoke to it saying, "Leg, you might not work, but you are coming along for the ride. The rest of me is moving on with or without you!"

It was the sweetest sight I had seen in a long time—the trail left in the snow from a leg that was unable to function. I was determined to make it with or without my leg's help.

As I walked, tears rolled down my cheeks and fell like drops of rain, landing in the soft snow beneath my feet. They were tears of victory. They tasted sweet as they trickled down my cheeks into my mouth. They were precious tears.

Sometimes it's the private victories we experience in our personal lives that are far sweeter and more meaningful than the public victories.

I kept up the "step and drag" program and remained committed to achieving my ultimate goal of running again for 45 minutes per day. Each day I studied subjects related to nutrition, vitamins, natural cures, and remedies. I became an investigator looking for ways to improve what I had left after the accident. I eventually got to the place where I was running a half hour per day.

I practiced annunciating my words and avoided using certain words that I had difficulty pronouncing and that caused me to stutter. I rehearsed them over and over until I mastered them.

Hey, I wasn't back in the game for a full three periods but at least I was off the bench.

I began speaking again and tested my limitations. On one occasion, I agreed to do a full day workshop. By mid-afternoon, my brain knew what I wanted to say, yet the connection from my brain to my mouth just didn't happen. It sounded as if I was drunk. I spoke to the person who had hired me and asked, "Can we take a break and I will give the group some interactive exercises to do together? I am in the process of recovering from a major accident with a head injury, and I need to back off a bit."

They were gracious and understood.

I explained the exercise to the group, handed out the sheets, and took a break. I went out of the room, took out my all-natural "cognitive enhancers," drank a greens and protein shake, went back into the room, and finished the day.

I learned that I was not ready yet to do a full day training session at this point in my recovery.

Today I am able to jog forty-five minutes a day, lift weights, and maintain a healthy dietary and nutritional supplement routine.

The Seven Secrets to Handling Life's Hurts

Major setbacks can be effectively managed. Here are some real-world principles for handling them when they come your way.

1. Don't rush the process of pain.

It may be physical or emotional pain that you are experiencing, or both. Sometimes, we have to go through this process of realizing how bad our situation is before we crawl up and out of it to look at the possibilities. In time, you will learn how to take a kick in the gut, feel the pain, and continue to persevere. Sometimes it feels as if you have had your heart ripped out and you have been left bleeding all over the place. You can't stop the bleeding no matter how you position your hands to apply pressure. The pain just seems to flow every day; and there is nothing you or anyone else can do to stop it. The next step is to move from focusing on the pain, to getting a plan together to make the best of what you have left. It is learning to focus on what you have left rather than what you have lost. It is transforming the pain into a constructive breaking point experience and moving forward.

This process takes different time frames for each of us. Life's painful events can either make us a "bitter" person or a "better" person. We can either walk through life as an angry victim asking, "Why me?" or we can let the process of pain shape us into a more compassionate, empathetic, and stronger person. I do believe that learning to keep moving ahead in spite of your pain builds perseverance and the stuff of which champions and top achievers are made.

2. Learn how to manage your negative self-talk.

Seventy-seven percent of what we say to ourselves is negative in nature. Sometimes that hits the 90% mark when we experience a major setback in our life. One of the best ways to manage our negative self-talk is to relabel what it is we are experiencing in order to diminish the emotional intensity connected to the words we use to describe how we feel. I remember how I would feel discouraged when I focused on how I would stutter. I would say to myself, "Who would ever hire a speaker who stutters? Nobody will ever want me." I then looked at my stuttering in a new context and said to myself, "I will just

tell people I have PPS—Porky Pig Syndrome—
Bedip, bedip, bedip, be dats all folks!" I would
blame my years of watching Porky Pig for my
stuttering since he was my role model! I changed
my unresourceful feelings connected to my stuttering by putting it in a humorous light.

Did I stop stuttering?

No.

However, instead of using negative self-talk
and making myself feel depressed, I diminished
the negative emotional intensity by reframing it
with the use of humor connected to Porky Pig.

3. **Realize that sometimes as you are in the process
   of achieving your goals, life gets in the way.**

Just this morning, I woke up feeling somewhat negative. I then changed my focus by asking
myself the question, "What can I do to get out of
this state? What has worked before?" I looked
forward to getting on the treadmill for a run and
then working on this book. My outlook began to
improve.

After getting off the treadmill, I went to put
on my newly purchased $400.00 glasses I had
left on top of the air hockey table. I went upstairs
and searched for them. They were nowhere to
be found. Then I noticed an odd-shaped piece
of twisted metal which looked like a form of
abstract art lying on the kitchen floor beside the
dog's food dish. They were my glasses!

Our dog, Oreo, had stood up on his back legs, stretched himself out over the air hockey table, and grabbed my glasses. He took them upstairs where he could enjoy chewing them undisturbed.

My brand new $400.00 glasses were destroyed. Oreo, who is part Australian Shepherd and part Border Collie, had a wonderful time using them as a chew toy!

Sometimes we can learn how to manage our emotional states and outlook on life; however, we can't prevent things from happening in our lives. Life happens. Setbacks happen. The unexpected happens.

4. Do the best with what you have and where you are. Then improve upon it.

I like to call this, 'Go with what you have left'. When you face an unexpected situation, start focusing on what resources you have left rather than on what you have lost. Make the most out of what you have left and enhance them to their fullest capacity.

My car broke down the day before Christmas, and my youngest son, Michael, and I were stranded at the side of a rural highway. I didn't have the cell phone with me and there were no houses in sight. It was also very cold out, and the wind was howling.

I looked in the trunk and found a survival kit I had put in the back of the car in case of an emergency.

Michael seemed scared and nervous; the temperature began to fall quickly. In the kit, I had gum, candies, flares, some basic first aid supplies, a lighter, and candles. I also had those space blankets that look like tin foil. I wrapped Michael up in the blanket and lit a couple of tea light candles and set them on the dashboard.

"Hey, Michael, we are going to have a party!" I said.

We divided the candy and pretended we were just camping out for awhile. We talked about how someone might stop to help us and that we had enough candles to keep us warm until help arrived.

Soon someone I knew came up, banged on the window, and helped us out.

Michael learned the principle of doing the best you can with what you have and where you are—even if you don't have much.

5. Challenge the so-called 'experts'.

Sometimes, you have to challenge the prophetic utterances of others who tell you that whatever it is you want to have or accomplish is impossible. When you face a major setback in your life, you are often vulnerable and often look to the experts for help.

Sometimes they are wrong.

I came across a listing of a few "experts" and here is what they had to say:

"This telephone has too many shortcomings to be considered as a means of communication. The device has no value to us." — Western Union internal memo, 1876

"Heavier-than-air flying machines are impossible." — Lord Kelvin, President, Royal Society, 1895

"If I had thought about it, I wouldn't have done the experiment. The literature was full of examples that said you can't do this." — Spencer Silver on the work that led to Post-It note pads

"We don't like their sound, and guitar music is on the way out." — Decca Recording Co. rejecting The Beatles, 1962

"I think there is a world market for maybe five computers." — Thomas Watson, Chairman of IBM, 1943

6. See every setback as an opportunity for a comeback.

When the unexpected happens you will feel the shock; you will feel the pain. It may throw you off your game for awhile while you regroup.

Then, come to the place of breaking point once again and turn the situation around. Use your setback as an opportunity for a comeback. Surprise the critics, the experts, the naysayers, and those who thought you had been knocked down for the count.

Frank Sinatra said, "The best revenge is massive success."

I'm not saying you hate those who have hurt you or attempted to stop you from working on your dream.

I am saying that you can reframe negative experiences and use them to motivate yourself to achieve your goals—to prove to those who thought you would amount to nothing that you are capable of making something out of your life.

Rebuild what you have left and move on despite how you feel some days. Push yourself through the bad days; and, in doing so, making it through them the next time will get just a little bit easier as you develop perseverance.

Thomas Edison's Dreams Go Up in Smoke

Thomas Edison received a phone call in the middle of the night informing him that his plant in Orange County was going up in flames. Edison, his wife, and his son got in their car and drove to the site. Edison and his son got out of the car and watched as the building burned.

"Go get your mother. She needs to see this," Edison told his son.

He stood there with his wife and son watching the blazing fire climbing ever higher into the sky.

"Isn't this something. We will never see a fire like this again. Look at those magnificent flames!" said Edison as he watched his blueprints, plans, and prototypes from years of research literally go up in smoke.

The next day while Edison and his son were walking through the rubble, Edison bent down and picked up the charred remains of a prototype he had invested years of time and money into developing. His son thought Edison was about to cry as he held the charred remains in his hands.

Edison stood up and said, "Thank God. Thank God. Thank God. All our mistakes have been burned up, and now we can start anew!"

Edison did go on to rebuild his factory and went on to invent the world's first phonograph, as well as thousands of other inventions.

No matter what happens in our lives, we can make the choice. We can become bitter or better. Better people handle life's setbacks. How? They realize that it is never too late to start a new beginning.

7. Ask yourself 'discovery' questions.

When you encounter a setback, ask yourself the following questions:

What have I learned about myself?

What have I learned about others?

What will I do from now on as a result of this experience?

What might I have done differently to prevent this?

How many different ways can I turn this adversity into an opportunity?

Successful people are often those who have failed the most. They are those who have often been hurt the most. They are those who have often been disappointed the most. However, the one key trait every successful person possesses is the ability to carry on toward the achievement of their goals despite adversity.

Personal achievement is not reserved for the intelligent, the good looking, or those who have all the right connections. As you examine the lives of top achievers, you will discover that their perseverance in spite of adversity and their ability to not be controlled by their 'feelings' are the predominant key character qualities they have developed over time.

Chapter 10

Distractions

"He who would arrive at an appointed end must follow a single road, and not wander through many ways." – Seneca

Have you ever been to the circus? Have you ever seen the lion tamer inside a cage cracking his whip with one hand while holding a three-legged stool in his other hand?

I have always wondered why the lion didn't simply lunge forward and devour the guy who was yelling at him and cracking that whip.

I came across some interesting information connected to this mystery. Apparently, the lion doesn't even think about his tremendous strength and ability to overpower the lion tamer.

Why?

The lion is distracted by attempting to focus his eyes on all three legs of the stool at the same time. This keeps him confused and unable to realize that he could simply bypass the small wooden stool and eat the lion tamer. The legs on the stool distract him from realizing the massive potential he possesses, and therefore it keeps him enslaved to the trainer.

Watch out for three-legged stools!

Four Reasons Why We get Distracted

The moment you begin to make a significant change in your life, or begin to work toward the achievement of a specific goal, it seems like a million and one distractions enter your life.

Why?

Let me give you four reasons I believe we encounter distractions the moment we decide to take action and actually do something about changing our lives.

1. Subconsciously we are resisting change.

It could be that there is a destructive part of us or a lazy part of us that wants to stay where we are in life. It is a self-sabotage system that we put into motion to prove to ourselves that the negative beliefs we hold about ourselves and our potential is true.

For example, we may say to ourselves, "I never complete anything I start." We then subconsciously start looking for distractions that we can use as excuses for not getting the job finished to reinforce such a negative belief.

2. Distractions test our commitment.

In some weird way, it seems as if life wants to really test our commitment to the goal we have set for ourselves. I can't explain it. Haven't you noticed that the day you choose to start eating nutritious foods and watch what you eat, is the day everyone in the office is invited out to the 'all you can eat' Chinese food buffet—and the company is paying for it?

3. Distractions come from others who subconsciously don't want us to change.

Have you noticed that your children, who usually sleep in, are all of a sudden awake at 6:00 a.m. the very first morning and every morning thereafter once you commit yourself to walking on the treadmill at 6:00 a.m. every day?

Have you noticed that you are all of a sudden expected to stay late at work the day after you enrolled in evening classes to advance your career?

Have you noticed that as soon as you reach the point of enjoying the fruits of your achievement, someone in your family becomes ill or is in crisis and requires all your attention?

Have you noticed that as you begin to make positive changes in your attitude and in your life, those in the office with whom you once had a good relationship are now banding together to sabotage your career?

4. Distractions are the result of not setting boundaries.

Setting boundaries with others means being firm with them in terms of you getting the solitude you need to get things done.

It seems strange that whenever you set boundaries with others, the more they seem to interrupt you.

Eight Ways to Effectively Manage Distractions

D - Don't give up!

Realize that you might be distracted every time you plan to work on your goals. Learn to laugh at it and realize that life is testing you. Once, while working on a project, I could predict the exact moment I was going to be interrupted. I wasn't practicing self-fulfilling prophecy; I just intuitively knew. I would say out loud, "Now, bang on my door. Right on cue and action!"

Sure enough I would be interrupted. I would then laugh to myself, refocus, and carry on.

I - Invent ways to avoid being distracted.

Once, I parked my car at the back of the building so people driving by wouldn't stop into my office to tell me all their troubles. It was amazing. People would bang on the office door, and when I opened it they would say, "I didn't see your car out front, but somehow I knew you would be here."

S - See some distractions as a sign of people wanting to know they are loved or recognized.

Sometimes those closest to you will distract you from what you are doing since they subconsciously want you to stop what you are doing and focus your attention on them. They want to know if they are more important to you than whatever it is you are working on.

T - Talk to yourself.

Transform a negative into a positive. You may say something like this: "The louder the kids play their music on the computer, the more and more focused I become working on finishing what I have started."

R - Review where, when, and how you get distracted.

Notice the patterns that distractions seem to take in your life. Recognize who, what, when, where, and why? Identifying specific distractions that take place will assist you in coming up with a plan to either manage them more effectively or avoid them.

A - Allocate a specific time and place to accomplish what needs to be done.

Let people know that this is your time and your space. Make it the same time and same space on a consistent basis. Train the people in your life to know that you are simply not available at this time and when you are in a particular space. Create time and geographical anchors that people become accustomed to.

C - Control your emotions when distracted.

Have you ever blown up at the kids when they have constantly interrupted you as you were working on something?

Yeah? Afterwards, how productive is your work as you feel guilty for losing it with your kids?

Develop walk away power—the power to walk away from the situation when you are ready to lose your emotional control. When you are unable to walk away from a situation, see it as if you are looking down upon it as an outside observer. Learn how to detach yourself from situations in which your emotional buttons are pressed.

T - Train yourself to stay focused on your goal instead of being lured into all the 'great opportunities' that will come your way.

Sometimes the 'good' can be the enemy of the 'best'. Once you get moving toward your goal, it will seem like a thousand new and wonderful opportunities will cross your path.

You will be tempted to give up your original goal and pursue all these other 'time limited' opportunities.

Do you know why new opportunities present themselves to us once we have decided to commit ourselves to achieving a specific goal?

I believe we look for them, and we are open to attracting them into our lives in order to justify giving up on the goal we committed ourselves to achieving. We move from one good opportunity to another, seldom accomplishing anything, and seldom achieving the best for ourselves.

Chapter 11

Motivating Yourself to Succeed

"Success means having the courage, the determination, and the will to become the person you believe you were meant to be." – George Sheehan

Motivating yourself on a consistent basis is the key to reaching your goals and making the changes you want to see happen in your life actually become a reality.

Positive self-motivation involves using a set of skills we can all learn in order to keep ourselves from relapsing and falling back into the old rut.

Positive self-motivation means discovering exactly what it is that will drive you toward the accomplishment of your goals.

Everyone is Motivated by Something

There is a story about a Texas millionaire who, while having a pool party at his estate, told his guests, "I know that every man is motivated by three things — money, power, and pleasure. I have filled my swimming pool with hungry sharks, and whoever dives in the pool and swims from one end to the other will be rewarded. They can either have one million dollars in cash, the position of president in one of my companies, or my beautiful daughter's hand in marriage."

All of a sudden, there was a "splash" as a young man dove into the pool, swimming with all his might to make it across to the other side through the shark-infested water.

He climbed out, gasping for air, breathing heavily, and lay on the deck. The Texas millionaire asked him in front of all the guests, "Tell me, son, what you want? Do you want the money? Do you want to be president of one of my companies? Do you want to have my beautiful daughter's hand in marriage?"

"I don't want any of those things, sir," he gasped while catching his breath.

"Then what do you want?" asked the millionaire.

"I just want to know the name of the guy who pushed me into the pool!" he answered.

External Motivators

External motivators may include cutting out a picture of what it is you desire to look like, have, do, or become.

External motivators also may include other people who are either using praise or pain to push you toward change or achieving some goal.

When we depend upon external motivators such as other people, most of the time we simply do things "because they want us to succeed".

External motivators can be used to get you to the place of breaking point to change. They can be used to give you a mental picture of what possibilities might exist for you and your life. Sometimes external motivators become less important to us as we develop internal motivators that drive us to achieve.

Internal motivators are often the offspring of progress and achievement. Once we see the outcomes and results we want to achieve, we often discover an internal motivation to continue.

For example, a sales representative has the external motivation to make more money through commissions if they sell more product. However, in time, they may become somewhat addicted to how it "feels" inside of them to see their name published in the company newsletter rather than focusing on the money they are making. Seeing their name in the newsletter and being recognized by their peers begins to internally motivate them more than their increased earnings.

Simply knowing they are at the top of their game and staying there becomes their new internal motivation for doing well. They become addicted to the "feeling" inside more than the money in their wallet.

Internal Motivation and Self-Actualization

Internal motivators are often connected to our value system and our deepest desires. We want to change for the better since something inside of us pushes us to move ahead.

It is not all about the money. It is not all about the recognition or freedom we might gain if we achieve our goals.

It is all about living up to our potential. It is all about knowing and believing that we can be more, have more, and do more in our lives.

Internal motivators are linked with deeper needs within us that we know must be met if we are to move ahead on the pathway of self-actualization.

What is self-actualization?

Self-actualization is moving toward becoming the best we can be. It means identifying, accessing, and using our potential. It means to continually be moving forward, living out our lives in our fullest capacity in the moment, and continuing to grow.

Most people who are not on the road to self-actualization are often depressed, frustrated, angry, bored, complaintive, critical of others, and may have addiction issues.

People who are not on the road to self-actualization may sell themselves out for lesser goals and dreams.

Instead of identifying, accessing, and using their potential, they remain 'stuck' where they are and make their lives as interesting as they can by doing whatever they can to create some form of challenge or excitement that may be either constructive or destructive in nature.

They sell out to the small wins among small-minded people whom they interact with in their own micro-kingdom.

Internal Motivators Linked to Our Passions

A person might be tired on Friday at 5:00 p.m. when they leave the office. They might have been negative and complaintive about their boss and everyone they work with all week long. However, at 7:00 p.m. that same Friday evening when they are teaching people how to make their own remote controlled airplanes, they are vibrant, positive, mentally alert, and energetic. They can stay up until 1:00 a.m. drinking coffee with others who share the same interests and amazingly not be tired the next day.

Why?

They have an internal motivation fueled by their love for something that is linked to their unique drive and interest.

When people are doing what they are passionate about, they come alive despite how tired they might have been or how stressed their day was. Have you ever noticed how your partner may be "too tired" to help you clean up the yard at 7:00 p.m., yet they come alive wanting to be intimate with you when you go to bed just after the 11 o'clock news?

There is no such thing as time or a clock when people are internally motivated and who are in harmony with their unique purpose in life. Those who are living out the purpose for which they were created lose all track of time when they are doing what they love and were created to do.

How to Discover Your Own Internal Motivators

1. Do you ever recall a time in which you felt totally in "the zone" in terms of being completely in harmony with yourself when engaged in some activity?
2. Has anyone every approached you about something that you did that left a significant positive impact on their life?
3. Have several people ever told you throughout your life, "You should be a ____" because you have a natural gifting for it? What did they suggest you become?
4. If you did not have to be concerned about money, what would you want to do with your life?
5. Think about different times in your life when you felt as if you were operating at your maximum potential. Do you notice any patterns emerging?

6. What would you change or accomplish in your life that would give you the greatest sense of personal satisfaction?

7. If you thought about those who ridiculed you, rejected you, or hurt you in some way, what significant positive changes could you make in your life that would override the wound and replace it with a great feeling of accomplishment and satisfaction?

8. How would you define a "sweatless victory"? Something you would enjoy doing so much it wouldn't even seem like work to you? Something positive that you could become addicted to—like the good feelings it generates within you when you engage in the activity?

Further Exercises You Might Consider

I - Identify

Imagine yourself achieving your dream and then inviting all those who attempted to sabotage you, all those who had ridiculed you or hurt you in the past, to attend a banquet in which you congratulated them for helping you develop the internal motivation to succeed. See yourself thanking them for being "divine teachers in disguise" as they were used to help you develop an internal motivation to overcome their negativity and influence.

Identify how you would feel after doing this.

N - Needs

Ask yourself the question, "What are my deepest needs?" See beyond your present circumstances and your present situation. For example, you may think you need more money. Your deeper need might be to use your unique gifts that are in harmony with your life purpose. As you use them, often the money you need will come.

T - Track

Track moments in your life when you were so engrossed in doing something that you were completely unaware of the time. These moments may help you gain insight into some of your internal motivations and your deeper needs.

E - Explore

See life as a buffet table and explore your options in terms of being open and receptive to new ventures. Sometimes, while sailing in uncharted waters, we make new discoveries about ourselves and what drives us internally.

R - Reason

Attach reasons to why you want to accomplish specific goals. Make a list of both your external and internal motivations before you begin setting your goals.

N - Notice

Increase your sense of personal awareness and notice how you feel after you do something. At one time, I conducted seminars on an annual basis on the subject of death and dying. It was three years later that I noticed I was depressed for about two months after holding the seminars. The subject of death and dying did not harmonize with my life's purpose.

A - Accept

Accept your uniqueness and be careful not to conform to those around you, sacrificing your internal motivation for the sake of approval and acceptance of others.

L - Let Yourself Live

Live out your unique purpose in life and live in harmony with your unique design. We are at our best when we are moving toward being the best we can be.

Chapter 12

Overcoming Negative Self-Talk

℘

> "Seventy-five percent or more of everything that is recorded and stored in our subconscious minds is counterproductive and works against us—in short, we are programmed not to succeed!"
> – Shad Helmstetter[8]

There is a story about a man who worked for the railroad who inspected the box cars each night to make sure they were locked.

One night while he was in a refrigerated boxcar, the door became jammed, locking him inside. Although he did everything he could to open the door, it would not open. He cried out for help, yet no one heard him. Finally, he slumped down beside some boxes and resigned himself to his fate of freezing to death.

Pulling a marker out of his pocket, he wrote on the wall of the boxcar a brief chronological account of the last few hours of his life.

He wrote the following:

11:00 p.m. – starting to feel very cold
12:00 p.m. – losing feelings in my limbs
 2:00 a.m. – feeling my body beginning to shut down
 3:00 a.m. – freezing to death. I love my family. Goodbye. I am dying.

In the morning, around 9:00 a.m., when the next shift had arrived, they opened the jammed door to the boxcar to find the man lying dead on the floor.

An investigation took place that same day.

The investigation revealed that a wire had somehow become disconnected in the refrigeration unit of the boxcar. Due to this, the boxcar could only produce cold air at a temperature of 66°F—a temperature that would not cause anyone to freeze to death.

The man in the boxcar interpreted his situation as being life threatening. He had told himself he was going to freeze to death and through his own self-talk he made it a reality in his life.

What is Self-Talk?

Self-talk is what we say to ourselves either out loud or internally. For example, you may drop something and say out loud, "I am so clumsy and awkward!" Perhaps you may be informed by your boss that there is room for improvement in terms of adding more graphics to your presentations. You then tell yourself inside your own head, "I can't do anything right. I always mess up in everything I do." These are examples of internal self-talk.

Replaying the Past

Self-talk also includes replaying in our minds the negative declarations others have spoken over us and into our life. Most of us can freshly recall all of the negative and critical statements others have made about us. We tend to focus on these rather than the positive ones.

One of the best ways to manage these negative self-talk statements made by others in our past is to change the internal voice we hear inside our head as we listen to them.

For example, take the words of criticism and destruction spoken over you and hear them in the voice of Elmer Fudd from the Bugs Bunny cartoons.

By doing this, you will alter and possibly diminish the negative emotional and psychological intensity when you replay the statements in your own mind.

Your Self-Talk Creates Your Identity

What we say about ourselves, either out loud or to ourselves in our own heads, shapes our identity. If you say to yourself, "I'm so stupid," you will move toward losing your discernment skills and actually create and reinforce an identity of "being stupid".

If you say out loud, "I have a hard time losing weight and everything I eat goes straight to my hips," then you will move in that direction. You will be sending a message to your subconscious mind to store fat and place it on your hip area. If you say to yourself internally, "Nothing ever works out for me. I always seem to fail," you will program yourself to walk into this identity.

Our subconscious mind accepts what it hears that is either negative or positive in nature. When we say things to ourselves, either out loud or within our own minds, we are giving direct commands to our subconscious mind to move us in the direction toward making what we say a reality in our lives.

Talking to Myself

Before a speaking competition, I once engaged in some serious negative self-talk. I had told myself in my own mind, "Who am I to be here? There is no way I will win this competition. Some of these competitors have been professional speakers for years. I am just a nobody from some little hick town who was lucky to get this far. Maybe they felt sorry for me. I'll try, but I probably won't win."

Then I began to think about the members of my club who had wished me well before I left. I recalled their words of encouragement and their excitement that someone from their club had actually made it this far in the competition. I looked at the little scraps of paper in my pocket that they had given me. They read, "Good luck, Norm. I know you will come back a winner!", "Make us proud, Norm, and blow them away!", "Just be yourself and you will win."

I was out in a back hallway waiting for them to announce my name to step up to the podium. I reached breaking point and said out loud, "That's it! I have come a long way and I didn't come here for nothing. I have come here to take back the trophy to my club. Who cares if the other guys are wearing thousand dollar suits? Who cares if they speak professionally? I'm going to blow them away. They will wonder, 'What little town is this guy from?' This is my moment. I can hear it now, 'And the winner is Norman Barlow.'"

I continued to talk myself up out loud, saying these things over and over again.

I heard someone inquire, "Is the next speaker ready yet?"

The coordinator replied, "I don't know if he is done talking to himself yet. Give me a moment and I'll see."

I didn't care who heard me talking aloud to myself. All I knew was that I had to get out of that place of being consumed with negative self-talk and change things around to create the outcomes I wanted.

By the way, I won the competition and spoke like a mad man, giving it everything I had. I went back to my home club and we all shared in the victory.

Talking Yourself Up

For years I have heard this self-esteem stuff about having other people 'build you up' and having a 'support system' or a group of people who will 'rally to your cause'.

I didn't really buy into it since I asked myself some key questions about this concept.

What if they leave you? What if they give up on you? What if you are no longer the 'flavour of the month'? What if they die? What if they use compliments and praise to control you and your feelings? What if they decide to withhold them? What if they are having a bad day right before your big game and fail to encourage you? What if they become jealous of your success? What if you are in conflict with them? Then you might be stuck in terms of feeling motivated when the curtain opens.

Learn how to talk yourself up. Become your biggest fan. Learn how to speak out loud those positive affirmations that will move you toward getting the outcomes you desire.

Quit looking for someone else to build you up and motivate you to move beyond your fears and feelings of negativity. Quit relying on others to pump you up and give you the power to make things happen.

When we depend upon someone else to motivate us and build our self-esteem, we are placing ourselves in a very dangerous position. Why? We often give them the power to determine our identity and our destiny.

We often only rise to the limits and expectations that others set for us.

Talking yourself up means speaking words of life and power into your own spirit that breaks the cycle of negative self-talk. It moves you toward self-reliance in terms of creating your own motivation rather than waiting for someone else to spoon feed it to you at their discretion.

Self-Talk Promotes Change

Tom Gullikson, a former tennis professional, had a challenge winning when facing a tie-breaking game. He lost almost every game when it was tied.

Gullikson had to reprogram his mind to manage tie-breakers more effectively.

He talked himself up by using the following strategies:

- He hung signs all over his house reading, "Gullikson loves tie-breakers."
- Throughout the day, he repeated out loud to himself, "Gullikson loves tie-breakers."
- In restaurants, he would write on napkins "Gullikson loves tie-breakers," while waiting for his food.

Gullikson went on to win nine out of eleven tie-breakers by talking himself into a new belief associated to tie-breakers.

How to Engage in Positive Self-Talk

Here are some techniques you can use that will help you manage negative self-talk and move you toward creating positive states through the use of positive self-talk.

Scripting Positive Affirmations and Reframes

Begin your positive affirmation statement with the words "I am" and keep them in the present tense.

- "I am releasing the extra weight from my body each and every day."
- "I am motivated more and more each day to accomplish my goals."
- "I am finding it easier and easier to focus my thoughts despite distractions around me."
- "I am becoming wealthier and richer with each minute that passes by, and abundance of all good things flows into my life."
- "I am stronger and much more capable to manage stressors that appear in my life."
- "I am experiencing feelings of sadness less and less each day and finding myself becoming more and more hopeful."

Reframing means giving something a new interpretation. Reframing can diminish the emotional intensity we attached to a particular experience.

Change "I am feeling very tired and weak" to "I am feeling unresourceful at this time."

Change "I am feeling sad and depressed" to "I am feeling as if I have a low energy period right now; however, it will pass, and I will pick up soon."

Change "I can't believe that they would do such a thing to me!" to "I am a little peeved at what they did, and human nature never ceases to surprise me!"

Change "I am feeling very discouraged and disappointed" to "I am feeling challenged by what has happened, and I am curious in terms of how I will resolve this situation."

Change "It's no use. Every time I try to make a change, I fail" to "I find it to be somewhat of an adventure to discover how I can move through this moment and discover a new way of doing things to create the outcomes I desire."

Change "No one is willing to help me or encourage me in terms of achieving my dream in life" to "I am grateful for any help others are willing to give me in terms of achieving my dream in life. However, I cannot rely on anyone to motivate me. I must learn to motivate myself and develop self-reliance."

Affirmations must be accompanied with action to reinforce their validity. Reframing is a skill that can be learned and practiced on a daily basis to help keep you from being swallowed up by negative self-talk.

Listen to Your Own Voice

After discovering which specific types of affirmations and reframes you need to program into your mind, record them on CD or cassette and listen to them each morning and evening.

Replacing negative self-talk with positive affirmations backed up by action and resourceful reframes is like pushing out the dirty water in a glass as it is displaced by clean, pure water which fills it anew.

Train yourself to focus on the positive in any given situation.

Talk to yourself internally using a different rate and tone.

I once asked a person who wanted to experience more joy in their life the following: "Tell me, if you were to describe your inner voice, your internal dialogue, the way in which you communicate with yourself, who would you sound like?"

They responded in a slow drawn out voice, "I would sound like Eyor off of *Winnie the Pooh*."

I then asked them, "What if you could change the sound, tone, and rate of your internal voice? What if you could simply imagine and hear a new internal voice talking inside your head—one that would make you feel like you were more joyful and optimistic? What would such a voice sound like?"

They went on to describe that their new "joyful" internal voice would sound like "Tigger" and how it would affect their emotions, their view of themselves, and their life in a positive way.

For example, when we wake up on a damp, cold, rainy day that is bleak and dreary, we may say to ourselves internally, "Oh my, what a rainy, depressing day." However, if we said to ourselves, "Hey, it's a little wet out today, but I am looking forward to making the best of this day even though it is wet outside" in an upbeat tone and using such a reframe, it can help keep us from having our emotions and potential outcomes for the day dictated by the weather.

Counteract Your Internal Critic

I call this the "It's possible, however" technique. When your internal critic attempts to tell you something and presents it to you as absolute truth, challenge such negative statements.

For example, your internal critic may say, "You always give up so easily." You then attack the destructive internal statement by responding in your own mind with, "It's possible; however, I managed to complete two degrees while working part time."

Something weird happens on a subconscious level. The internal critic is now disarmed as you counter attack its claim.

Identify Moments of Exception

Moments of "exception" are those times in which you thought and believed you were unable to follow through with something or pull something off. They are times when your negative self-talk was rampant, and you said something to yourself or did something to break the cycle, and turned things around in terms of changing your state and your outcomes. These were "exceptional" moments in which you overcame your feelings and your fears to accomplish the task before you; moments in which you pushed through your negative self-talk and achieved your goal or survived a difficult situation.

Make a list of the moments of "exceptions" and keep any tangible reminders connected to the moments that you can use to let your brain know that you were able to make it then, and you are able to make it now—whatever the situation you are facing.

Keep Your Fears to Yourself

Don't go around telling other people what you fear may happen in your life. Sometimes other people will feed into your fears and even provide some false evidence to convince you that what you fear will take place.

Keep your negative self-talk and your fears to yourself.

It is not so much what others have said to us or about us that keep us from achieving our goals in life. It is usually the things we say to ourselves that limit who we can become and what we can achieve.

Chapter 13

Self-discipline

"Discipline is the bridge between goals and accomplishments." – Jim Rohn

It seems as if self-discipline has become a dirty word in our age when most people expect everything to come to them easily and quickly. We have "instant weight loss pills," pills to block carbs and fats so you can "eat and cheat," and "get rich quick" schemes that will provide you thousands of dollars each month with "little or no effort". It also seems as if the "I will do it when I feel like doing it" attitude pervades in our society, eclipsing the thought of taking action despite the state we are in.

I think we have created a culture in which most people want and believe they deserve all the luscious fruits of success without wanting to rise early each day in order to plant, nourish, and maintain the vineyard.

For some, they believe the fruits of success and personal achievement will simply fall from the tree by some mystical means and roll downhill arriving at their doorstep with very little effort on their part.

Self-discipline and perseverance are two small seeds that we must plant into our lives before we see the fruit of success in anything we undertake.

Self-Sacrifice

Self-discipline means that we give up those passing and fleeting moments of temporary pleasure and instead choose to do those things that will lead us to the accomplishment of what we desire in the long term.

For years I had simply focused on getting speaking dates here and there. I knew that I would have enhanced credibility and be offered more speaking dates at a higher fee if I had a book published in a field in which I had specific expertise. However, the whole idea of waking up early in the morning, staying up late at night, and setting aside time on the weekend to write a book really didn't appeal to me.

I wanted to earn more money, command a higher fee, and share with others what I had discovered about the science of personal achievement, yet I just chose not to do what I needed to do in order to go where I wanted to go in life.

Why?

I simply did not want to make the sacrifices necessary to achieve my goal. I allowed myself to simply get lost in the daily routines of life. I wanted to spend time playing guitar, working out, going to movies, and sleeping in until 11:00 a.m. on a Saturday morning.

It was easy to find, look for, and wait for excuses to come into my life and pass before me like clouds moving through the sky to give me reasons why I could not set aside dedicated time to finish writing my book.

Nothing was written until I realized that sacrifices would have to be made. Sleep was sacrificed, leisure activities curtailed, missing out on some family events, and waking up early on the weekends to write had to happen before progress would be made.

Once I attended a conference accompanied by my wife who offered to finish typing my manuscript for this book. While I was at the conference, she was locked away in a hotel room typing for several hours and only taking short breaks. Time we could have spent at lunch, at the end of the day, and in the evening was sacrificed in order for her to get the job done.

The ventilation in the small hotel room was poor. There was no view and the lighting was dim. However, my wife worked throughout the day and into the evening, wearing only her pajamas while typing away. She sacrificed shopping time, work out time, and time relaxing while just taking a break away from the kids.

If you want to achieve your goals in life, sacrifices must take place.

Self-discipline is learning to say "no" to all the wonderful opportunities that come your way when you have set aside time to make progress toward the achievement of your goal.

Self-discipline means giving up your temporary desires in order to take consistent action toward the creation of your future destiny.

No Such Thing as Later

One of my sayings around our house is, "There is no such thing as later." Practicing self-discipline means giving up the belief that you will do things later. Later doesn't exist. Later is a word that should be banned from the English language!

Whenever we say "I will do it later," we are not practicing self-discipline. We often wait for some good reason to come along that we can use as an excuse not to do the thing at all. Self-discipline brings with it a sense of urgency. Self-discipline carries with it a steady beat that keeps you marching toward your goal.

Those who are self-disciplined ask themselves, "What opportunities might be coming up that I can use to my advantage to progress toward the achievement of my goal?" The undisciplined ask themselves, "What's taking place in my life right now in order for me to put off doing what I need to do to change my life until there is a more convenient time — a time when I may 'feel like doing it'?"

Pushing Through the Pain

I like what Jim Rohn had to say about discipline. He said, "We must all suffer one of two things: the pain of discipline or the pain of regret or disappointment."

Self-discipline often involves pain. It involves continuing to do what you know must be done on a daily basis or in the magic moments of life even though you may be in a state of discomfort or you simply just don't feel like doing it.

It means 'sucking it up' before the big game or even during the game when things are not going your way or when things are unfair. It means putting your emotions on hold just for the moment to get the job done. It means choosing to keep the commitments you have made to yourself to accomplish what you have set out to do even under tremendous pressure from all sides.

I recently met a coach of a young women's university basketball team. I asked him what he did to get the results he was achieving with his winning team. He said, "I told them when it comes to winning the championship, I don't care about how many boyfriends left you or what is going on at home. It is all about focusing on making each pass; making each shot count. You let all the other stuff just fade away while you are in the moment. Then, after the game you can go back to all that stuff. I tell them to leave their baggage in their gym bag."

It seems as if those who are able to remain self-disciplined and focused make an identity shift in order to get the job done. They seem to zone out of that head space of being consumed with their personal and family issues, and morph into the person they need to be in order to do what needs to be done.

In times of mental anguish and emotional pain, most people simply give in and give up. However, teaching ourselves to push through the mental and emotional pain, to stay the course, and to continue on despite how we feel is crucial to not only achieving our goals; it is essential in building our level of self-trust and self-confidence.

It creates a voice within us that says, "Sometimes the winds of change and adversity blow. I may be knocked down, but I will rise up again and refuse to be knocked out!"

Self- discipline is essential to moving forward through time, making steady progress toward the achievement of our goals despite our setbacks and disappointments.

Self-discipline creates an inner trust that transforms into an awareness that even in the difficult times in life you know you will choose to get back to doing whatever it is you know you must do on a daily basis to experience the realization of the outcomes you want to achieve. It is key to developing self-confidence. Self-confidence is knowing that we can trust and believe in ourselves and our ability to produce specific outcomes in our lives despite our personal situation or present circumstances.

Life is Like a Mutual Fund

An investment advisor once showed me a graph of a mutual fund and its history. He discussed the performance of the fund throughout the years pointing out the times of high returns, average returns, and low returns. He then drew a line through the peaks when it yielded high returns and said, "As you can see, over the long term, despite the ups and downs of the fund, it has continued to make more and more money. Notice the line I have drawn through the time of peak returns, you can clearly see how the high returns outnumber the years the fund did not perform so well. In the end, it has proven itself to be a long term winner."

The mutual fund was a great metaphor for self-discipline. You and I will have our dips and dives. We will have our seasons of setbacks and relapses.

However, like a long term winning mutual fund, using the power of self-discipline we can ride out the storms and get back on track progressing toward the achievement of our goals.

Self-discipline sometimes involves forcing ourselves to do the things we need to do to secure the long term win. We all experience down times; times when we just want to run away and hide, eat bad food, and burn all of our motivational books and CD'S.

There are times when we choose to attend our own self made pity party and visit our own personal "hall of shame" and "hall of pain" reviewing old memories of what has happened to us or what might have been.

However, learning the art of self-discipline enables you to pull yourself through the slump and get back to doing what you know you need to do to win over the long term. It gives you a history, a track record, for you to look at and use to wake yourself up out of your slumber. Self-discipline gives you the power to act despite how you feel. It enables you to get going again and begin building back into your life the daily habits that will eventually produce in your life the results you desire to see take place.

Self-discipline Involves Re-dedication

Recently, I was following my workout routine and things were really moving along well. I then picked up some kind of a bronchial infection and a virus that left me feeling weak, tired, and unable to concentrate.

Everything went off the tracks. I began eating bad food, stopped exercising, and accomplished nothing.

I have been in this place before and knew that in time I would get over this virus or whatever it was and get back to doing the things I needed to do to keep myself in good shape. As soon as I started feeling better I re-dedicated myself to returning to my usual diet and workout routine.

I consciously chose one night before going to bed that tomorrow would be the day I returned to doing the things I knew I needed to do in order to re-establish my workout routine. I knew before I went to bed that it would happen tomorrow no matter what. I planned a gradual return to the lifestyle I once knew—a lifestyle consisting of habits I had developed over the years. That night before I fell asleep I knew the outcomes I would see at the end of the next day before that day had even begun.

Self-discipline gives you history to look back on, reference points and memories of times in the past in which you have "been here before". Memories of moments of self-discipline help you support your belief that it is possible to get back on track You can mentally replay previous comebacks and review how you got back into the game several times in the past.

Self-discipline does not mean we can be on top of our game all the time. It does mean that sometimes we get off track. However, we know from experience that it will not last. We also know that there is a moment in which we re-dedicate ourselves to getting back on track. We recognize it may take some time to get back up to speed; however, we choose each day to increase our velocity. Becoming self-disciplined in our lives gives us the security and self-trust to know that we can and we will get going again despite setbacks.

Doing What You Don't Like or Feel Like Doing

A lack of self-discipline is often why many gifted people have difficulty living out the type of life they have always dreamed of living. I once met an artist whose paintings were outstanding, and yet he was living in a hovel with barely enough to eat. He told me that in order for him to have his work recognized he would need an agent to represent him and that he did not know how to find one. I suggested he find a role model, another artist, who had an agent and ask them for advice.

"I don't have time to do that. I have my paintings to finish. I don't like meeting people and I would probably have to go to the city to get in touch with an agent anyway. I hate going to the city," he replied.

What kept an incredible artist living in poverty and being unrecognized? The lack of self-discipline. He simply did not want to pay the price to learn what he had to do in order to win at the game he wanted to play.

Discipline is doing the things you don't want to do in order to get to the place in which you can do whatever you choose to do.

Playing Out of Tune

I have seen local musicians play in battle of the bands contests in our community. Some of them are so excited about the opportunity to play before a live audience they fail to take the time to make sure their guitars are in tune together. The result is an absolutely awful sounding performance.

What would have made the difference between a good performance and a great performance? Self-discipline.

Taking the time to tune up their instruments ahead of time and then leaving them alone so they would not go out of tune before they walked on stage would have definitely affected the outcomes of the experience.

Self-discipline is putting your emotions on hold while continuing to do what needs to be done rather than being lost in the excitement, frenzy, or chaos of the moment.

Self-Discipline and Obscurity

Golf champion, Tiger Woods, had just finished winning the Masters in Augusta, Georgia.

People gathered around him afterwards and a gentleman asked him, "Son, what's it like to pick up a golf club and start whacking around those balls as well as you do?"

"Sir, I have been hitting balls for about nineteen years," replied Tiger.

"Nineteen years?" the older gentleman exclaimed. "Son, how old are you?"

Tiger Woods replied, "I am twenty-one, sir."

As soon as Tiger Woods was able to walk, his father, Earl, would teach him how to hold a club, how to putt, how to swing a club, and how to line up a shot.

Even when Tiger was in elementary school, he was memorizing the lay outs of golf courses around the world. He would see himself choosing the best club and carefully planning each shot before he had ever visited the green.

Self- discipline means focusing on the long term. It means taking the time to commit yourself to excellence. It means preparing yourself and whatever it is you will need or think you will need ahead of time before you arrive at your destination. Self-discipline often means training in obscurity and anonymity. Self-discipline is the key ingredient that often separates those who think they can win from those who know they can win.

Building Self-Discipline Into Your Life

Sometimes the best way to start building a positive character quality such as self- discipline into our life is to look back and reflect upon the times in the past when we have experienced it.

Ask yourself the following questions to discover those times in your life when you exhibited the qualities of a self-disciplined person.

- "When was there a time in your life that you made sacrifices in order to succeed at something?"

- "How did those sacrifices help you achieve your goal?"

- "What can you sacrifice and give up in your life right now that has been hindering you from working on achieving your long term goal? In what specific ways will this help you achieve your goal?"

- "When was there a time in your life when you did not feel like taking action, and yet you did so in order to achieve a desired goal?"

- "What were the positive outcomes you experienced by doing what needed to be done even though you did not feel like doing it?"

- "What is it that you really do not feel like doing now, and yet you know must be done if you are to reach your goal? What might be the positive outcomes if you actually finished the task?"

- "When were there times in your life when you 'sucked it up' and managed to reach your goal even though you were crying on the inside the whole time? What did you discover about yourself during that time?"

- "What personal pain or discomfort are you feeling right now that you know you must overcome in order to do what is necessary to achieve your goal?"

- "When were there times in your life when you experienced a setback and yet you made a comeback? When were there times in your life when you re-focused and re-dedicated yourself to starting all over again? When was there a time when you began doing the things you knew needed to be done in order to get you to where you wanted to be in your life? What did you learn about your ability to start over?"

- "In what way can you use your ability to start over right now?"

- "When was there a time in your life when everyone around you was drawn into the chaos and confusion, and yet you were able to remain calm and focused, keeping your thoughts and emotions under control? How were you able to do that?"

Visiting our personal "Hall of Fame" by reflecting on the moments of triumph in our past is a useful tool for building belief and confidence in ourselves to make positive and powerful changes in the present.

Chapter 14

In the End

℘

Well, we are at the end of our journey together and now you have a choice. You can choose to shove this book into a slot on your book shelf and say to yourself, "What an inspirational and entertaining read!"

You may choose to look for the next self-help book that has become popular and ask yourself, "I wonder what *they* have to say about the subject of personal achievement?"

You may choose to tear the pages out of my book and use them to line your bird cage, or perhaps you will use my book to share the interesting stories with others to entertain or inspire a group.

In the end, it's all about you.

What are you going to do with the strategies you have learned in this book?

Perhaps you will read this book over again and again.

Perhaps you will find it easier and easier to follow the step-by-step system to work toward the achievement of your goals.

Maybe you will decide to join us for one of our weekend workshops, drawing yourself away from your busy life in order to design the life you have always dreamed of living.

In the end, it comes down to making the decision to really changing your life for the better—becoming more, having more, and experiencing more of what life has to offer.

The only person who can make this happen is you.

Thank you for reading my book. Thank you for letting me share snapshots of my life with you. Thank you for investing the time and money to improve yourself.

Send me an email and let me now how things are going as you experience positive changes in yourself and in your life by using the skills, techniques, and strategies you have discovered in this book.

I look forward to hearing from you and eventually meeting you at one of our workshops or speaking events.

God bless you as you seek to discover His unique purpose and mission for your life. As you embark on your journey, let His purpose live within you and through you since there will never be anyone else just like you on this planet.

Bibliography

Bach, George R., and Torbet, Laura. *The Inner Enemy: How to Fight Fair With Yourself,* New York, NY: William Morrow & Company, Inc., Berkley Edition, 1985.

Bland, Glenn. *Success! The Glenn Bland Method,* Wheaton, IL: Living Books, Tyndale House Publishers, Inc., 1972.

Gerber, Richard, *Vibrational Medicine: New Choices for Healing Ourselves,* Santa Fe, NM: Bear and Company, 1996.

Helmstetter, Shad, *The Self-Talk Solution,* New York, NY: Pocket Books by arrangement with William Morrow & Company, Inc., 1987.

Helmstetter, Shad, *What to Say When You Talk to Yourself,* Scottsdale, AZ: Grindle Press, 1982.

Loehr, James E., and McLaughlin, Peter J., *Mentally Tough: Achieving Peak Performance in Business,* Don Mills, ON: Totem Books, 1987.

Murphy, Joseph, *The Power of Your Subconscious Mind,* New York, NY: Reward Books, 2000.

Robbins, Anthony, *Awaken the Giant Within,* New York, NY: Free Press, A Division of Simon & Schuster, Inc., 1991.

Robbins, Anthony, *Unlimited Power,* New York, NY: Ballantine Books, a division of Random House, Inc., 1986.

Endnotes

1. Kali Pearson, "Half Her Size," *Chatelaine*, January 2006 p.54.

2. Glenn Bland, *Success! The Glenn Bland Method* (Wheaton, Illinois: Tyndale House Publishers, Inc., 1972), p. 44.

3. H. Markus and P. Nurius, "Possible Selves," *American Psychologist*, Vol. 41, No. 9, September 1986 pp. 954-969.

4. Bill Phillips and Michael D'Orso, *Body for Life,* (New York, New York: HarperCollins Publishing, 1999).

5. Joseph Murphy, *The Power of Your Subconscious Mind,* rev. ed. (New York, New York: Reward Books, 2000), p. 22.

6. Laurence G. Boldt, *How to Be, Do, or Have Anything,* (Santa Barbara, California: Lightning Press in association with Ten Speed Press, Berkeley, California, 2001), p. 196.

7. Murphy, pp. 153-154.

8. Shad Helmstetter, *What to Say When You Talk to Yourself,* (Scottsdale, AZ: Grindle Press, 1982), p. 45.

Printed in the United States
93654LV00001B/175-303/A